大云山

西汉江都王陵1号墓发掘报告

（三）

南京博物院
盱眙县文化广电和旅游局　编著

主　编　李则斌
副主编　陈　刚　左　骏

文物出版社

北京 · 2020

EXCAVATION REPORT ON THE KING OF JIANGDU'S TOMB M1 OF THE WESTERN HAN PERIOD AT DAYUNSHAN

(Ⅲ)

by

Nanjing Museum

and

Xuyi County Bureau of Culture, Broadcast, Television and Tourism

EDITOR – IN – CHIEF：LI Zebin

DEPUTY EDITOR – IN – CHIEFS：CHEN Gang ZUO Jun

Cultural Relics Press

Beijing · 2020

彩　图

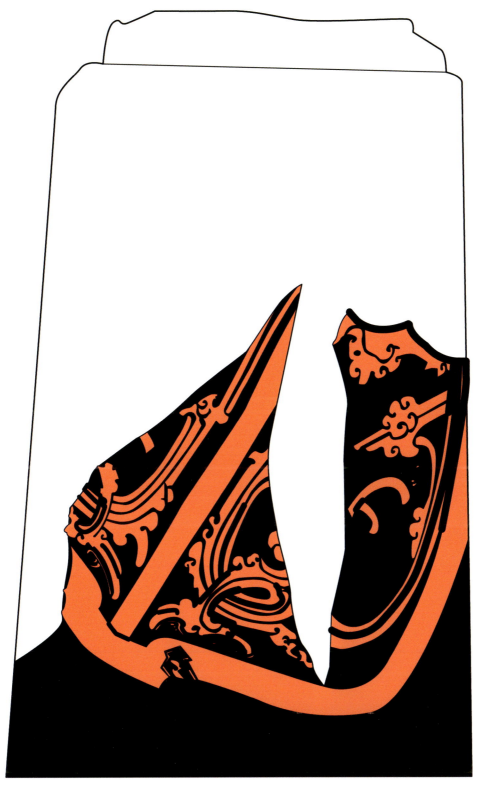

0   6厘米

彩图一 1号墓外棺残片

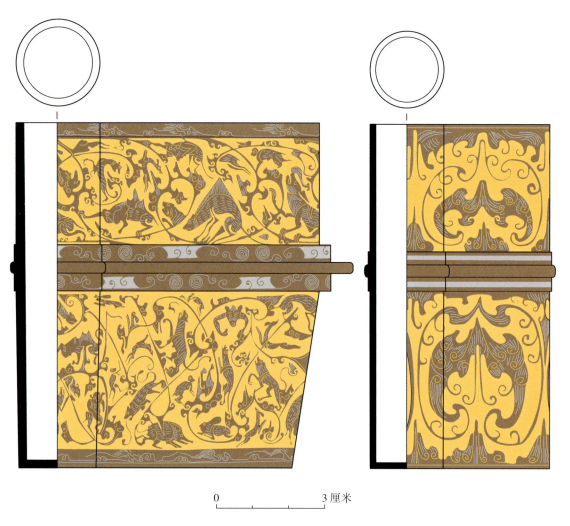

彩图二   M1DK⑥出土A型铜镦（M1DK⑥∶69）

0 3厘米

彩图三　M1DK⑥出土A型铜镇（M1DK⑥：553）

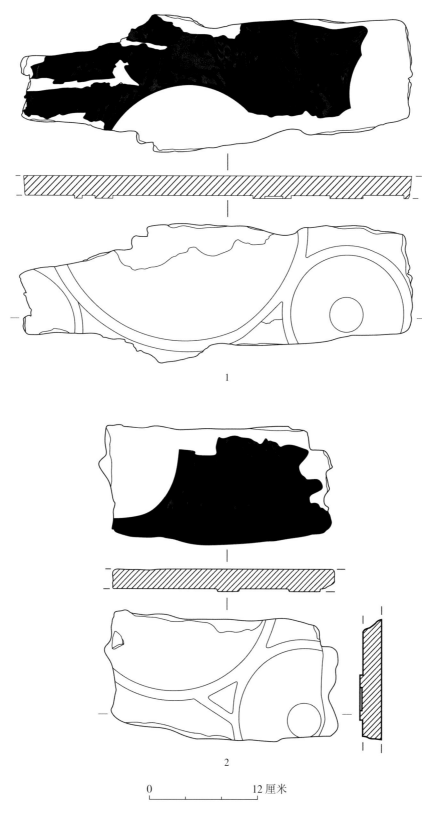

彩图四　M1DK⑥出土镶玉漆棺残片

1. M1DK⑥：434-1　2. M1DK⑥：434-2

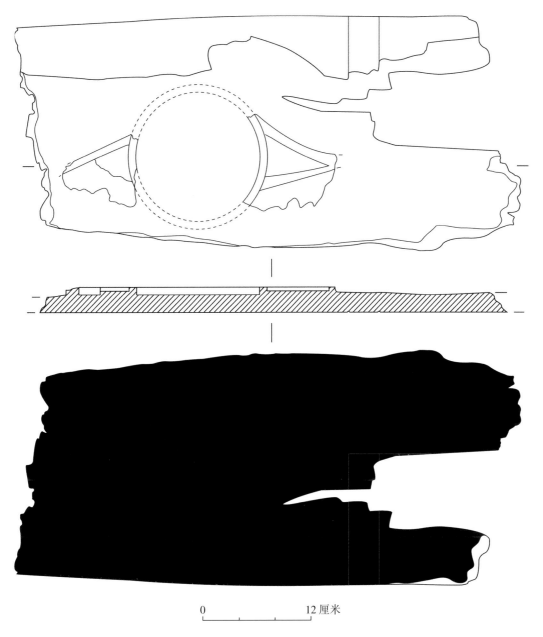

0   12厘米

彩图五　M1DK⑥出土镶玉漆棺残片（M1DK⑥：829–1）

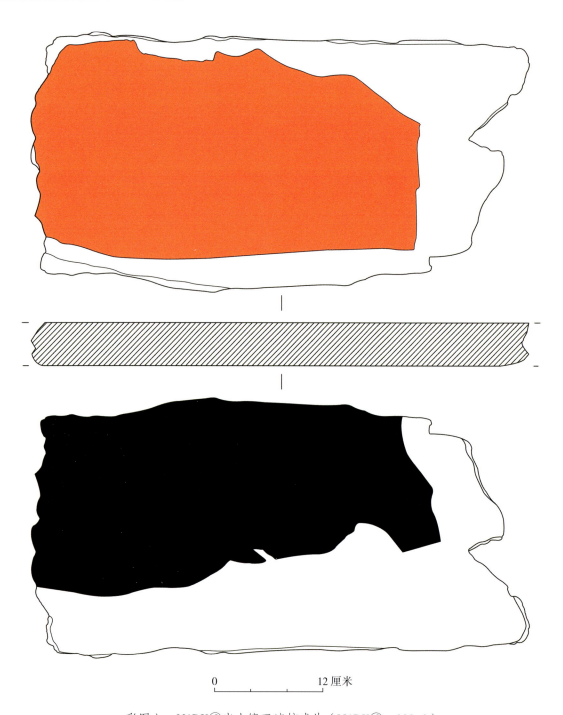

0   12 厘米

彩图六　M1DK⑥出土镶玉漆棺残片（M1DK⑥：829-2）

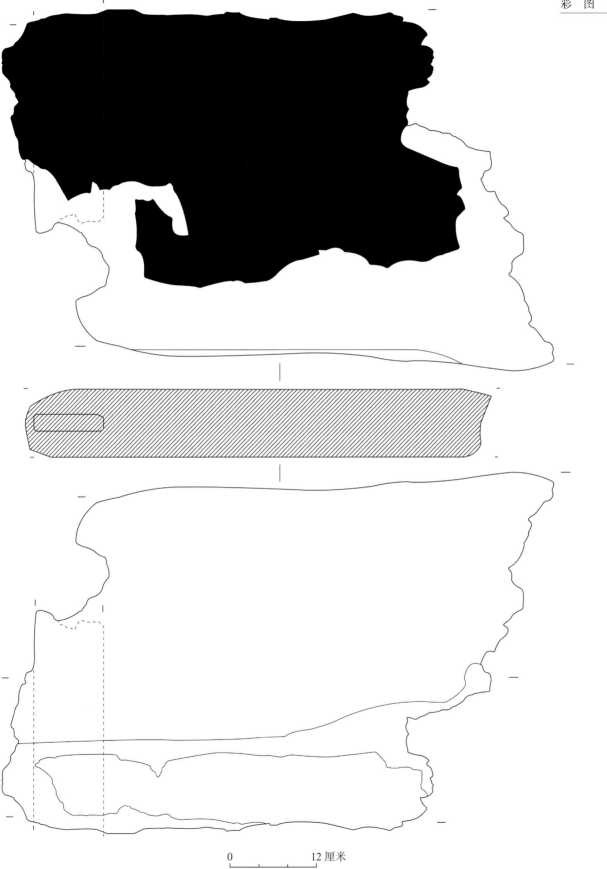

0　　　　　　　12厘米

彩图七　M1DK⑥出土镶玉漆棺残片（M1DK⑥：829-3）

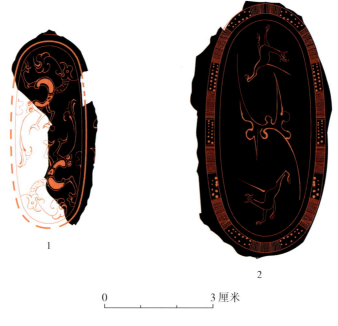

1

2

0 ————————— 3厘米

彩图八　M1DK⑥出土A型漆耳杯
1. M1DK⑥：595　2. M1DK⑥：1768

0   3厘米

彩图九　M1DK⑥出土C型漆奁（M1DK⑥：1404）盖俯视图

0 ⊢——⊢——⊢——⊣ 3厘米

彩图一〇　M1DK⑥出土C型漆奁（M1DK⑥：1404）盖内仰视图

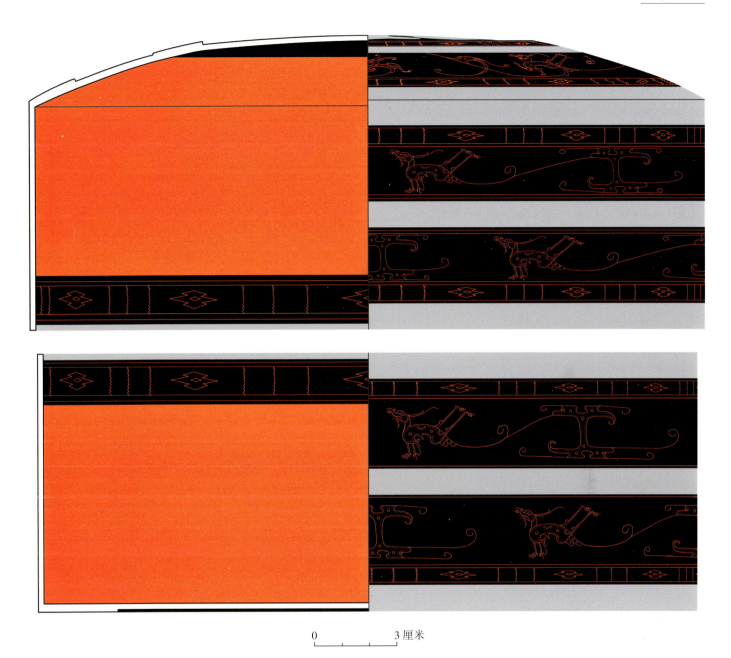

0   3 厘米

彩图一一　M1DK⑥出土C型漆奁（M1DK⑥：1404）

0 ⊢———┼———┤ 3厘米

彩图一二　M1DK⑥出土C型漆奁（M1DK⑥：1404）底仰视图

0   3厘米

彩图一三　M1DK⑥出土C型漆奁（M1DK⑥：1404）内子奁分布情况

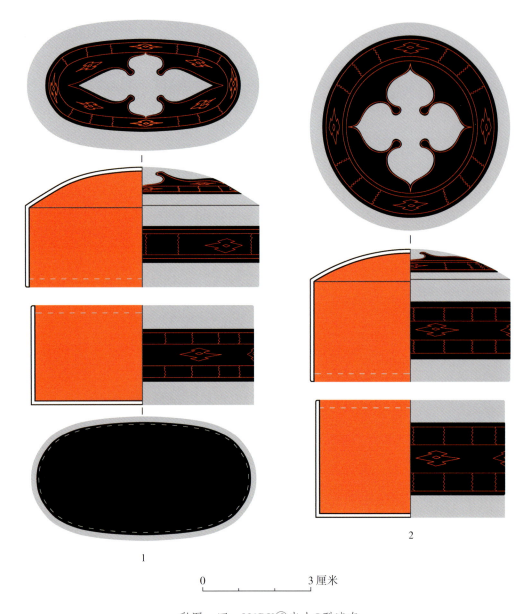

0   3厘米

彩图一四　M1DK⑥出土C型漆奁

1. 椭圆形子奁（M1DK⑥：1404-1）　2. 圆形子奁（M1DK⑥：1404-5）

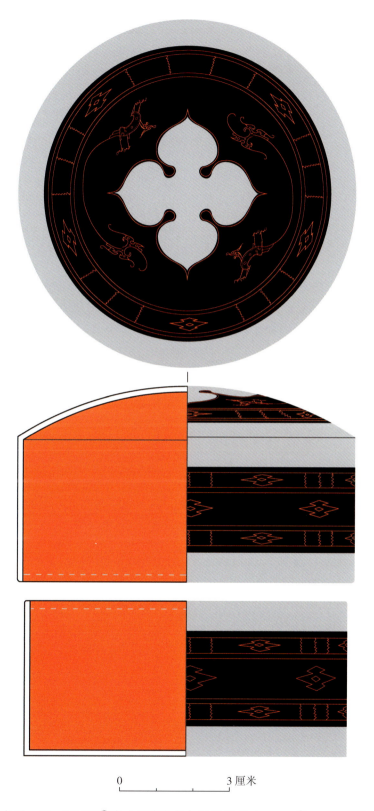

0   3厘米

彩图一五 　M1DK⑥出土C型漆奁内圆形子奁（M1DK⑥：1404-2）

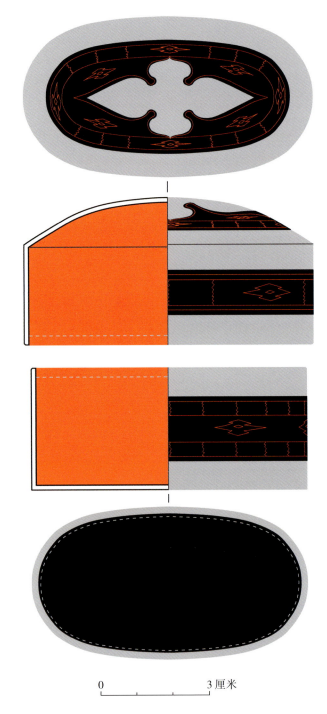

0   3厘米

彩图一六 M1DK⑥出土C型漆奁内椭圆形子奁（M1DK⑥：1404–3）

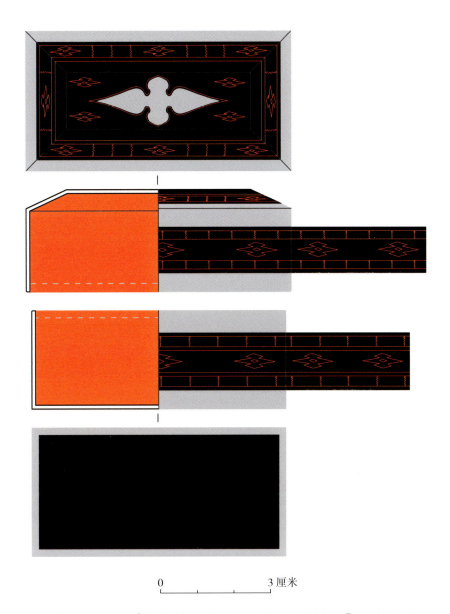

0   3厘米

彩图一七　M1DK⑥出土C型漆奁内长方形子奁（M1DK⑥：1404-4）

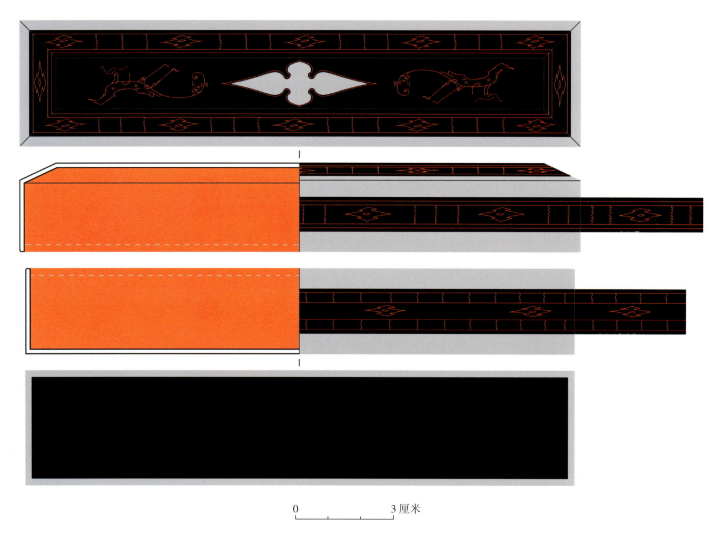

0   3厘米

彩图一八　M1DK⑥出土C型漆奁内长方形子奁（M1DK⑥：1404-6）

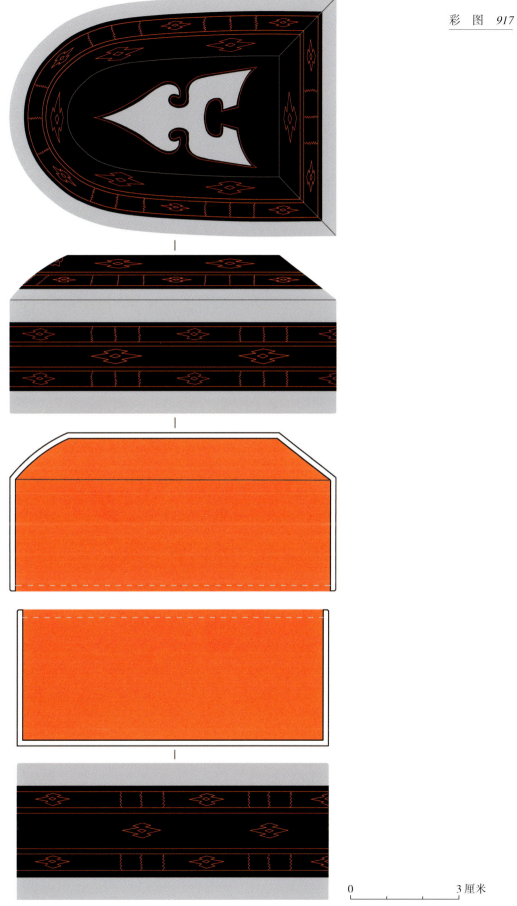

0   3厘米

彩图一九　M1DK⑥出土C型漆奁内马蹄形子奁（M1DK⑥：1404-7）

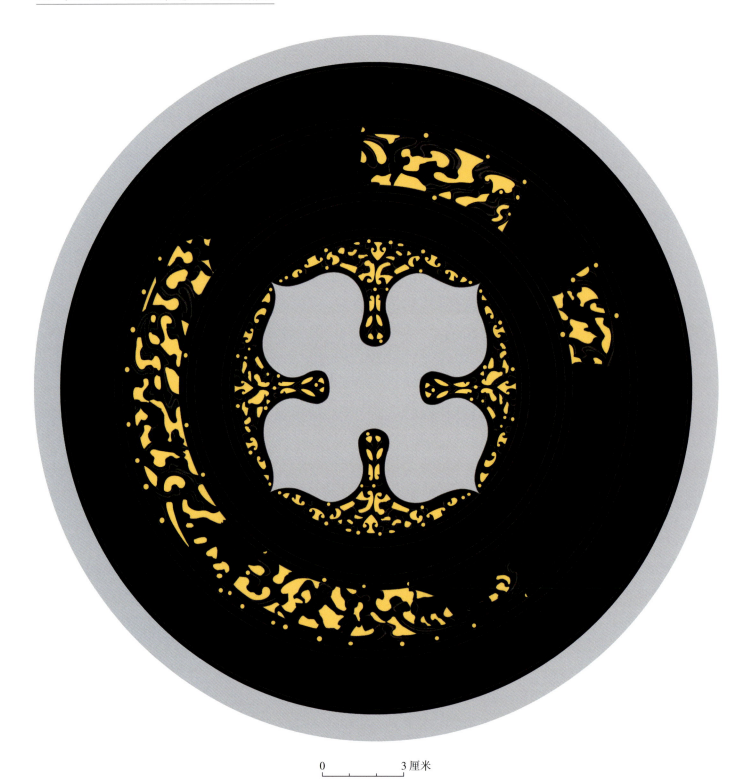

0 _____ 3厘米

彩图二〇　M1DK⑥出土C型漆奁（M1DK⑥：1402）盖俯视图

0   3厘米

彩图二一　M1DK⑥出土C型漆奁（M1DK⑥：1402）盖内仰视图

0   3 厘米

彩图二二　M1DK⑥出土C型漆奁（M1DK⑥：1402）底俯视图

0 _____ 3厘米

彩图二三　M1DK⑥出土C型漆奁（M1DK⑥∶1402）内子奁分布情况

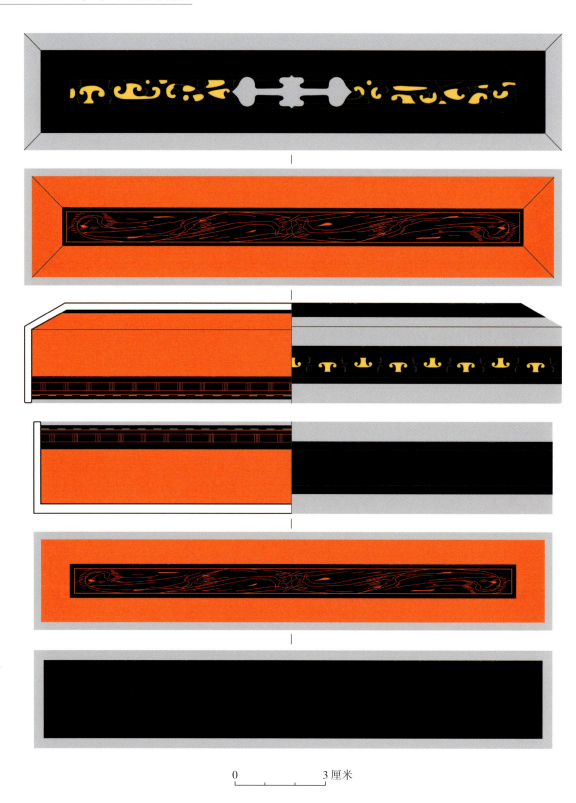

0 _____ 3厘米

彩图二四 M1DK⑥出土C型漆奁内长方形子奁（M1DK⑥：1402-1）

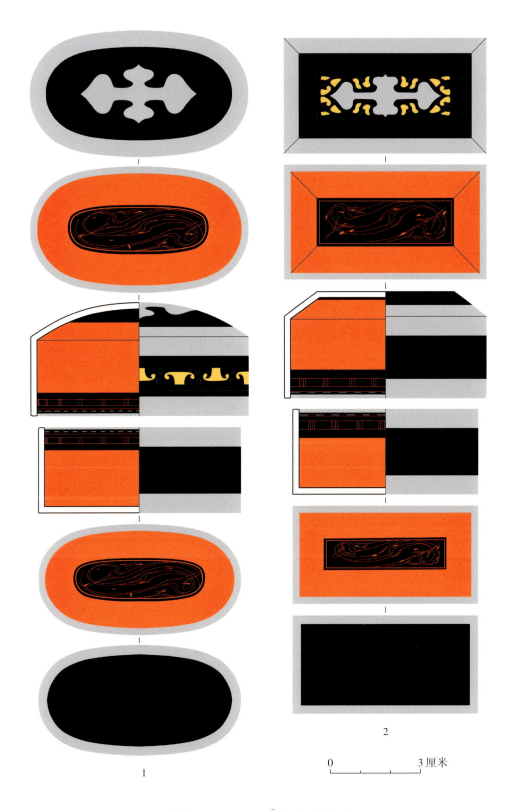

0 ———————— 3厘米

2

1

彩图二五　　M1DK⑥出土C型漆奁
1. 椭圆形子奁（M1DK⑥：1402-2）　　2. 长方形子奁（M1DK⑥：1402-3）

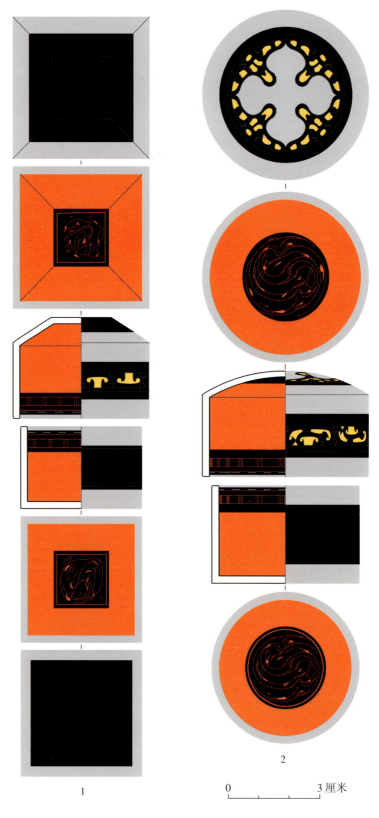

0   3厘米

彩图二六　M1DK⑥出土C型漆奁

1. 方形子奁（M1DK⑥：1402-4）　　2. 圆形子奁（M1DK⑥：1402-5）

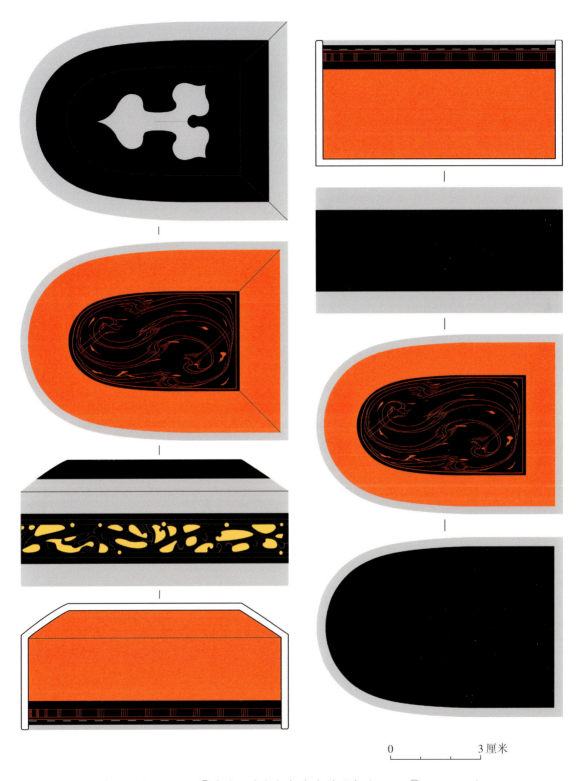

0   3厘米

彩图二七　M1DK⑥出土C型漆奁内马蹄形子奁（M1DK⑥：1402-6）

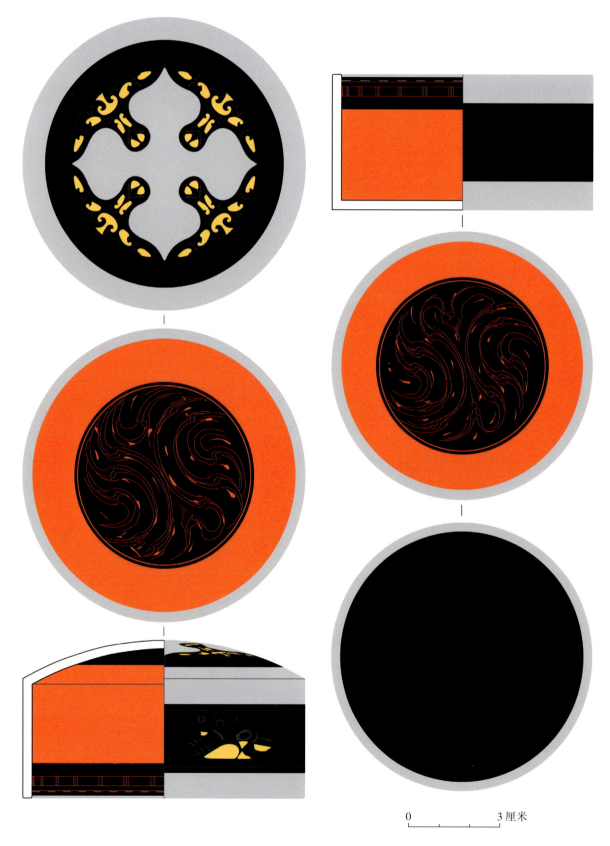

彩图二八　M1DK⑥出土C型漆奁内圆形子奁（M1DK⑥：1402-7）

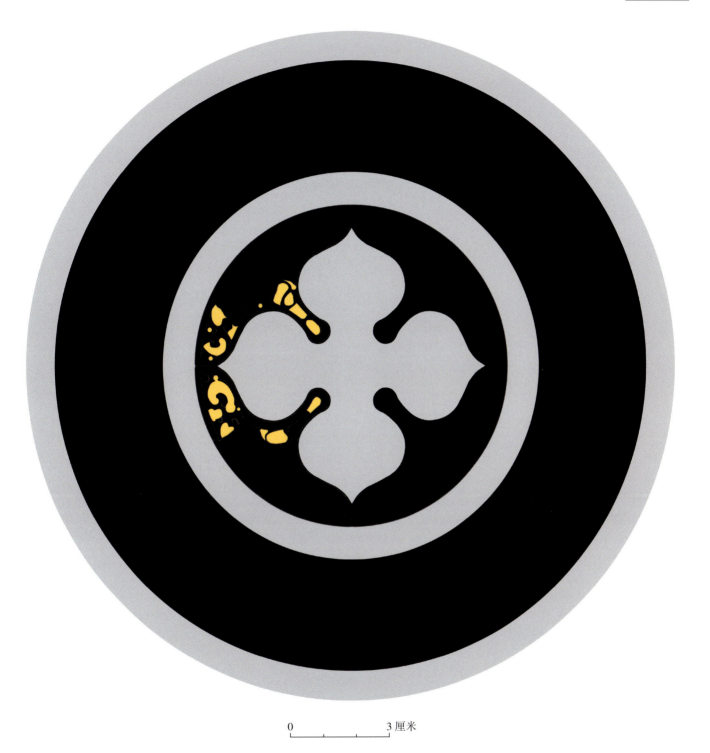

0   3厘米

彩图二九　M1DK⑥出土C型漆奁（M1DK⑥：1410）盖俯视图

0 ⊢———┴———┴———⊣ 3厘米

彩图三〇　M1DK⑥出土C型漆奁（M1DK⑥：1410）盖内仰视图

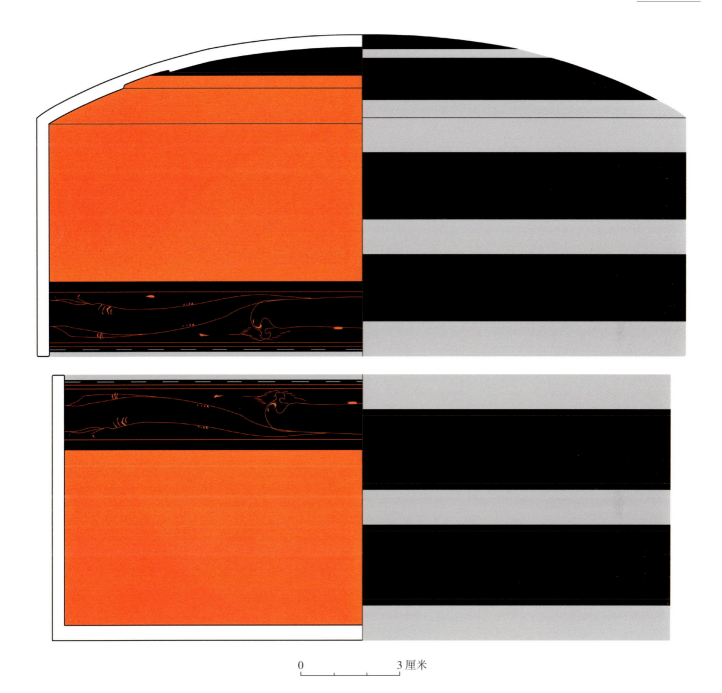

0   3 厘米

彩图三一　M1DK⑥出土C型漆奁（M1DK⑥：1410）

0　　　　　　　3厘米

彩图三二　M1DK⑥出土C型漆奁（M1DK⑥：1410）底俯视图

0　　　　　　3厘米

彩图三三　M1DK⑥出土C型漆奁（M1DK⑥：1410）内子奁分布情况

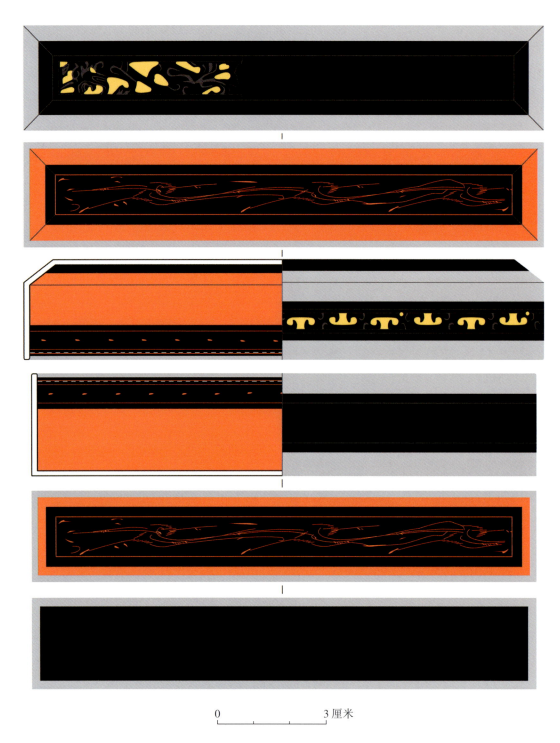

0   3厘米

彩图三四　M1DK⑥出土C型漆奁内长方形子奁（M1DK⑥：1410-1）

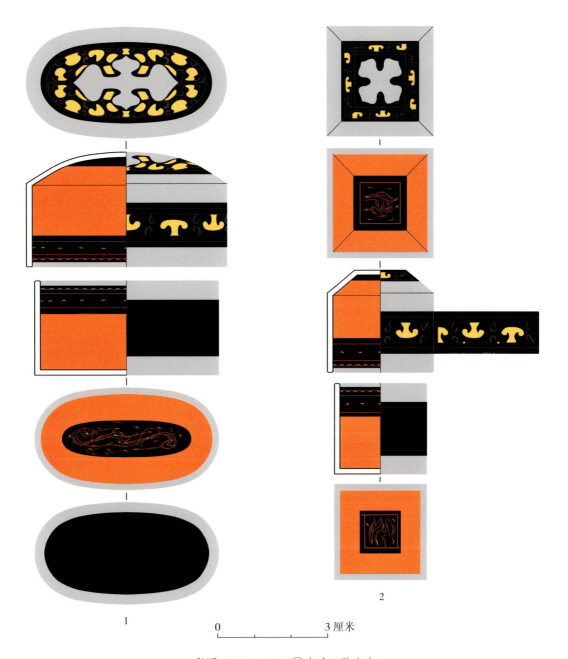

彩图三五　M1DK⑥出土C型漆奁
1. 椭圆形子奁（M1DK⑥：1410–2）　2. 方形子奁（M1DK⑥：1410–4）

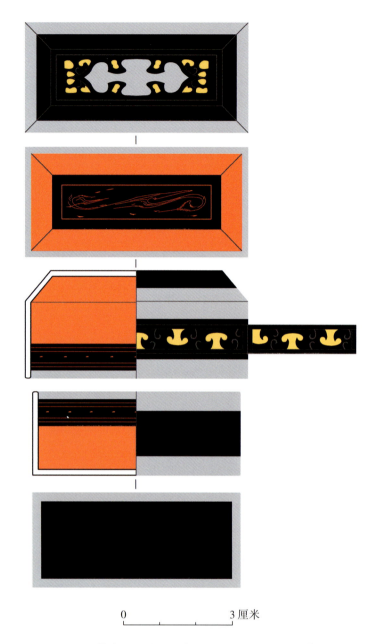

0   3 厘米

彩图三六 M1DK⑥出土C型漆奁内长方形子奁（M1DK⑥：1410-3）

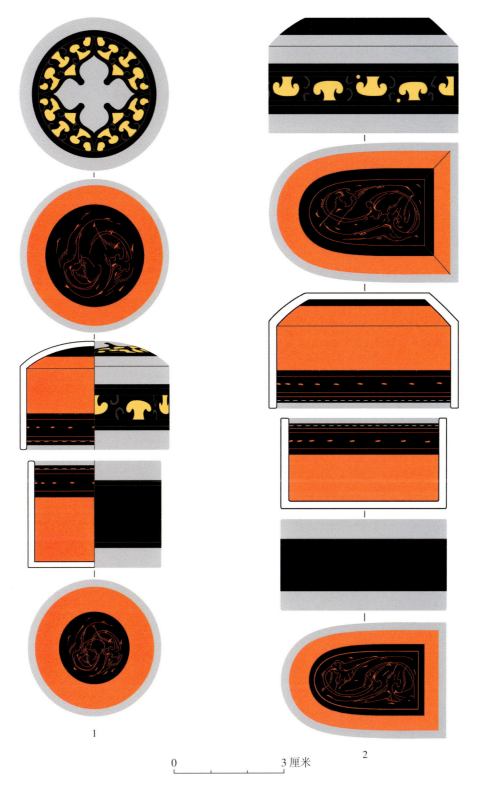

彩图三七　M1DK⑥出土C型漆奁
1. 圆形子奁（M1DK⑥：1410–5）　2. 马蹄形子奁（M1DK⑥：1410–6）

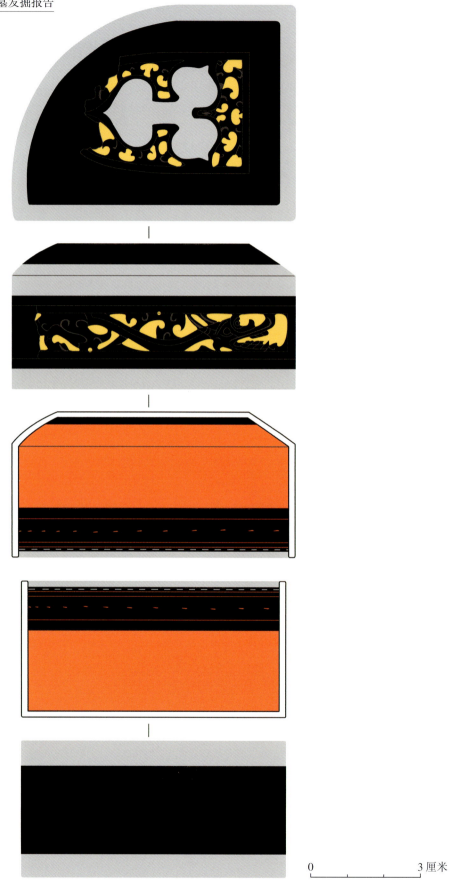

0   3厘米

彩图三八   M1DK⑥出土C型漆奁内马蹄形子奁（M1DK⑥：1410-7）

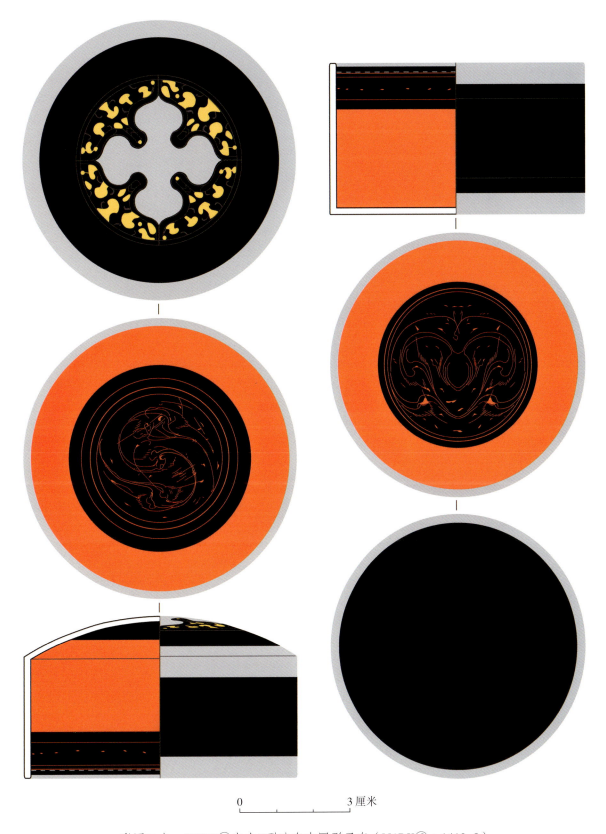

彩图三九　M1DK⑥出土C型漆奁内圆形子奁（M1DK⑥：1410-8）

0 ____ 3厘米

彩图四〇　M1DK⑥出土漆卮（M1DK⑥：356）

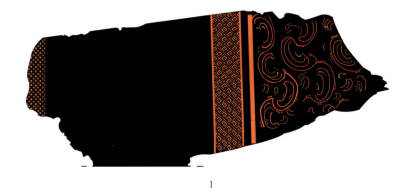

1

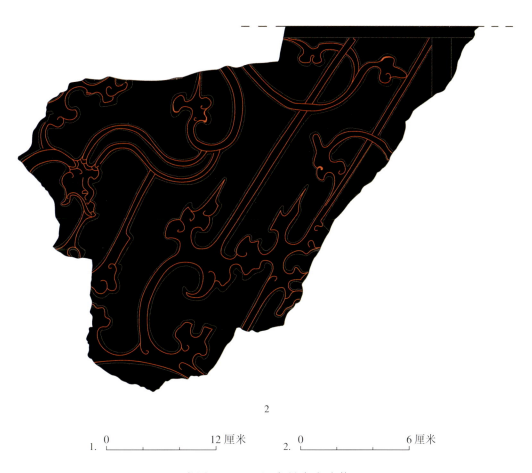

2

1. 0 ┄┄┄┄┄ 12厘米   2. 0 ┄┄┄┄┄ 6厘米

彩图四一　一区上层出土漆笥
1. M1Ⅰ：1662　2. M1Ⅰ：4972

0   3厘米

彩图四二   六区上层出土A型铜镦（M1Ⅵ：5111）

0   3厘米

彩图四三　六区上层出土A型铜镦（M1Ⅵ：5112）

1　　　　　　　　　　　　　　　　　　　　　2

0 ————————— 6厘米

彩图四四　六区上层出土E型铜镦
1. M1Ⅵ：5138　2. M1Ⅵ：5139

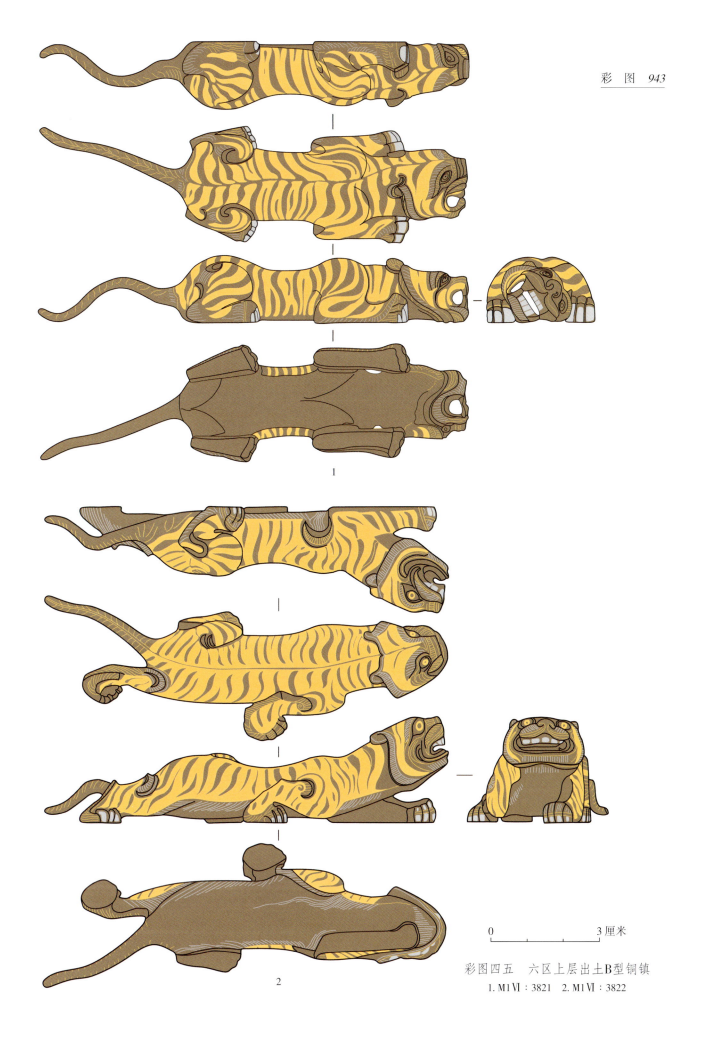

彩 图 *943*

0 3厘米

彩图四五 六区上层出土B型铜镇
1. M1Ⅵ：3821 2. M1Ⅵ：3822

1

2

0 　　　　　　　3厘米

彩图四六　六区上层出土B型铜镇（M1Ⅵ∶3823）

1

2

0 ⟼⟼⟼ 3厘米

彩图四七　六区上层出土C型铜镇
1. M1Ⅵ：5144-1　2. M1Ⅵ：5144-3

1

0   3厘米

彩图四八　六区上层出土C型铜镇

1. M1Ⅵ：5144-2 　2. M1Ⅵ：5144-4

0   6厘米

彩图四九　七B区上层出土乐器漆梁架（M1ⅦB：1764-1）

2

0   10 厘米

彩图五〇　一区下层出土铜虎（M1Ⅰ：3646）

彩图五一　一区下层出土漆沐盘（M1 I ：3744）

1.　0 ━━━━━━━ 6厘米

2.　0 ━━━━━━━ 12厘米

彩图五二　二区下层出土铜编钟（M1Ⅱ：3917）

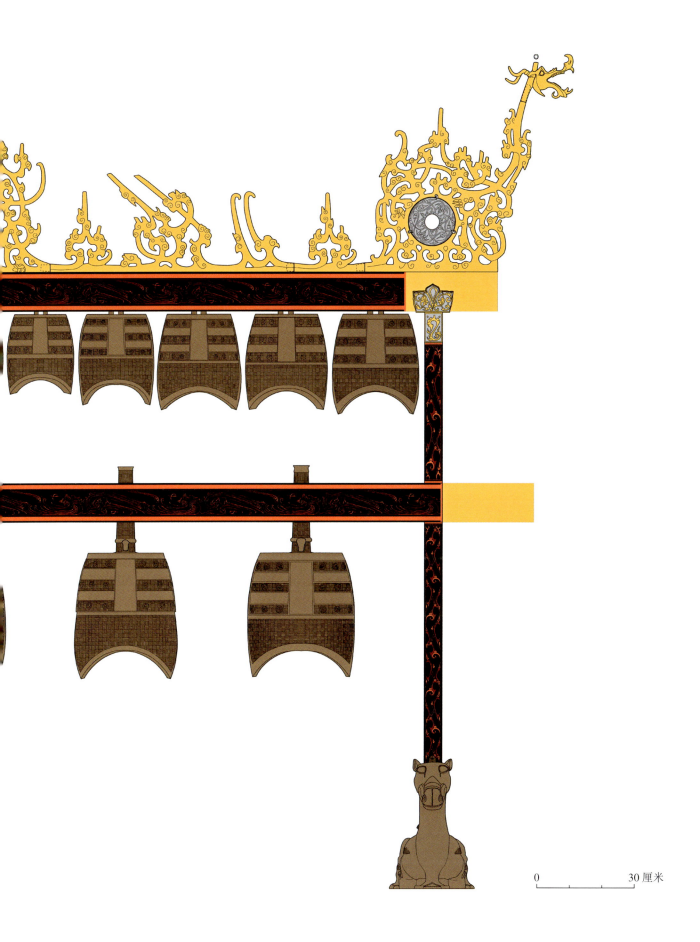

0 _____ 30 厘米

编钟上层横梁

编钟下层横梁

彩图五三　编钟横梁

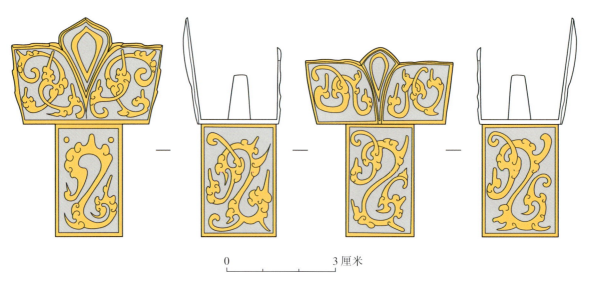

0　　　　　　3厘米

彩图五四　编钟托架（M1Ⅱ：3917-26）

编钟上层立柱　　　　　　编钟下层立柱

彩图五五　编钟立柱

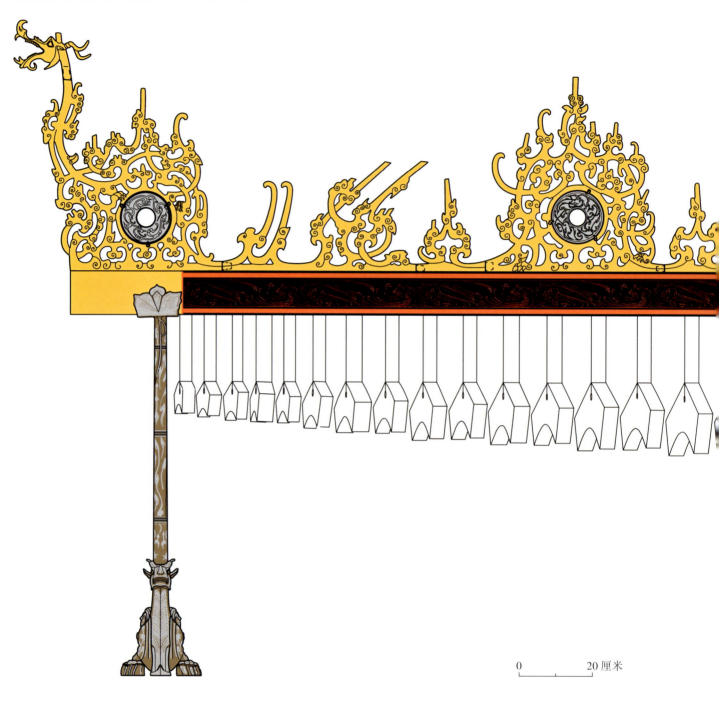

0   20厘米

彩图五六　三A区下层出土编磬（M1ⅢA：3918）

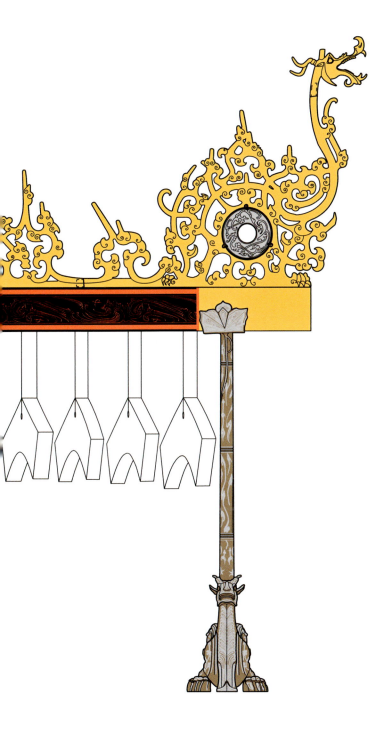

彩图五七　编磬横梁

0 　　　　　　　 20 厘米

彩图五八　三 A 区下层出土编磬铜底座（M1ⅢA：3918-21）

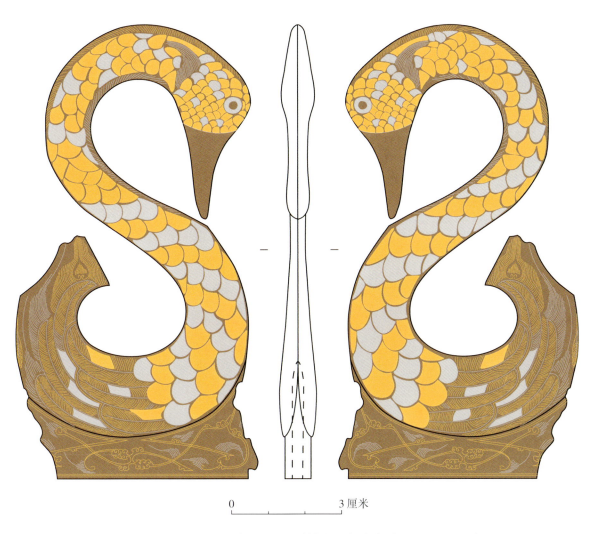

0　　　　　　　3厘米

彩图五九　三B区下层出土"S"形错金银铜饰件（M1ⅢB：3705）

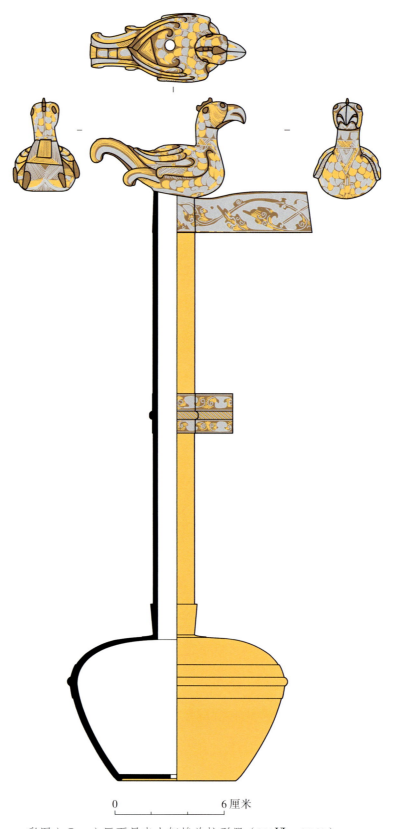

彩图六〇 六区下层出土铜鸠首柱形器（M1Ⅵ：3968）

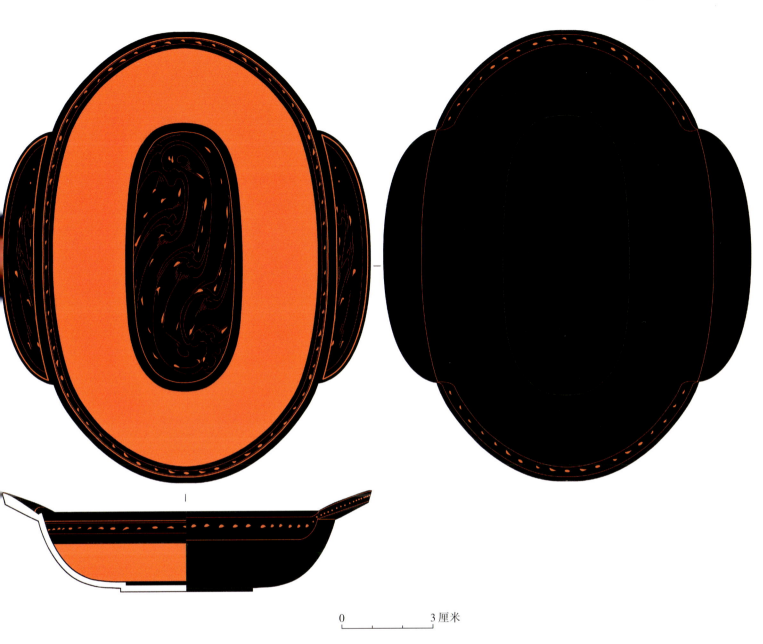

彩图六一　六区下层出土A型漆耳杯（M1Ⅵ：4627）

0 ⎯⎯⎯ 3厘米

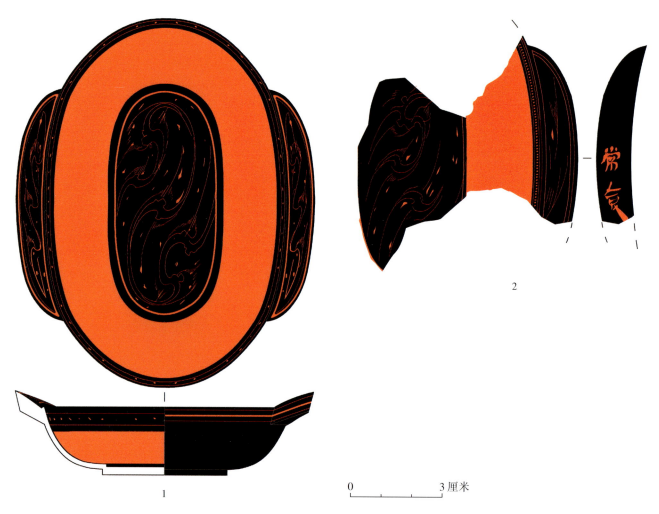

0   3厘米

彩图六二　六区下层出土A型漆耳杯

1. M1Ⅵ：4969　　2. M1Ⅵ：4626

0   3厘米

彩图六三 六区下层出土A型漆耳杯（M1Ⅵ：4916）

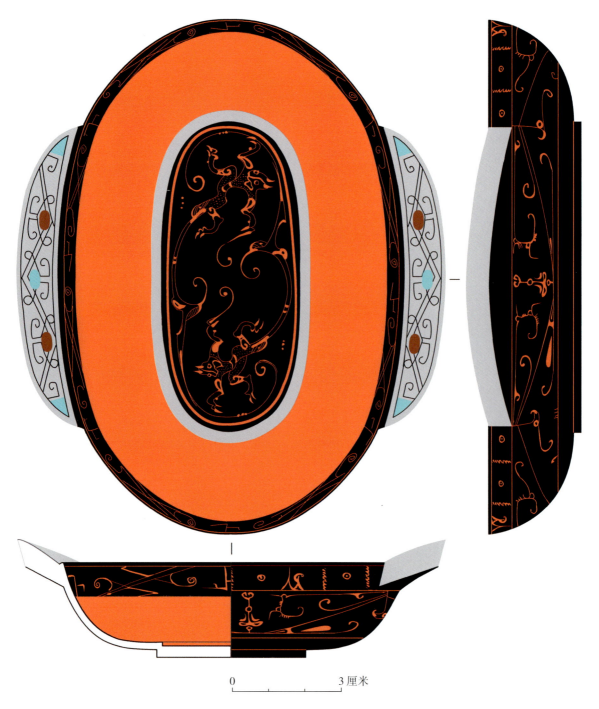

0 ⊢——————⊣ 3厘米

彩图六四　六区下层出土B型漆耳杯（M1Ⅵ：3853）

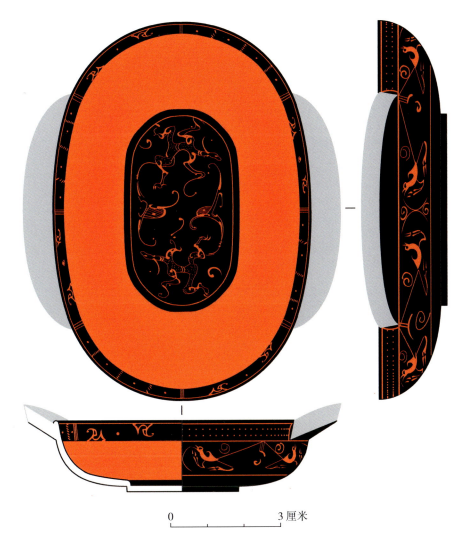

0   3厘米

彩图六五　六区下层出土B型漆耳杯（M1Ⅵ：4711）

0 ⊢——————⊣ 3厘米

彩图六六　六区下层出土 B 型漆耳杯（M1Ⅵ：5059）

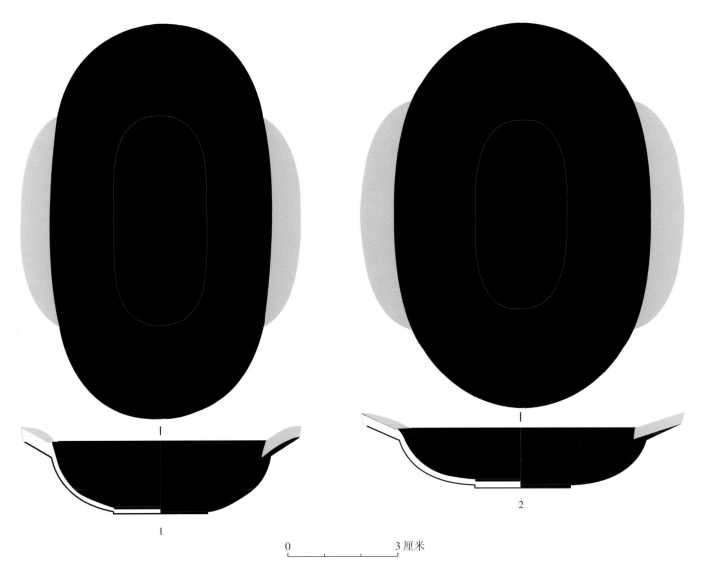

0   3厘米

彩图六七　六区下层出土C型漆耳杯

1. M1Ⅵ：4714　2. M1Ⅵ：4715

0   3厘米

彩图六八　六区下层出土D型漆耳杯（M1Ⅵ：4890）

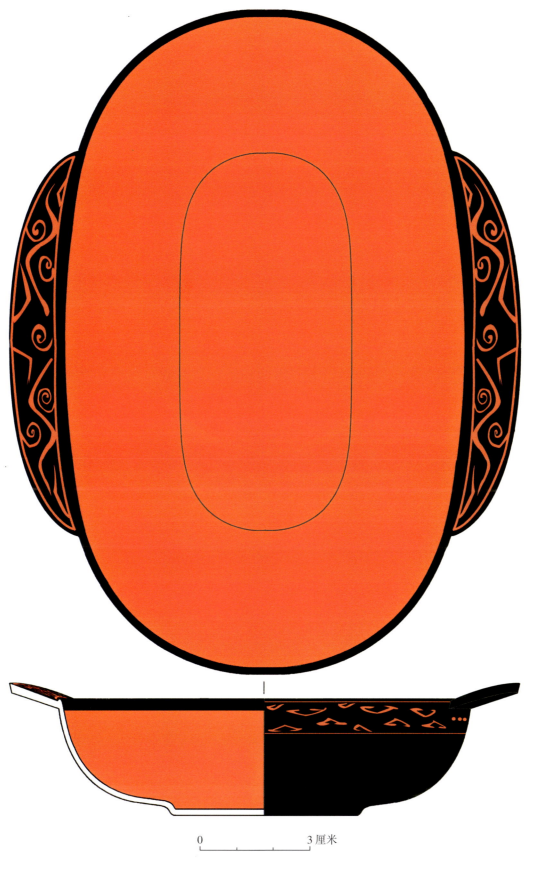

彩图六九　六区下层出土D型漆耳杯（M1Ⅵ：4896）

0   3 厘米

彩图七〇 六区下层出土 D 型漆耳杯（M1Ⅵ：4915）

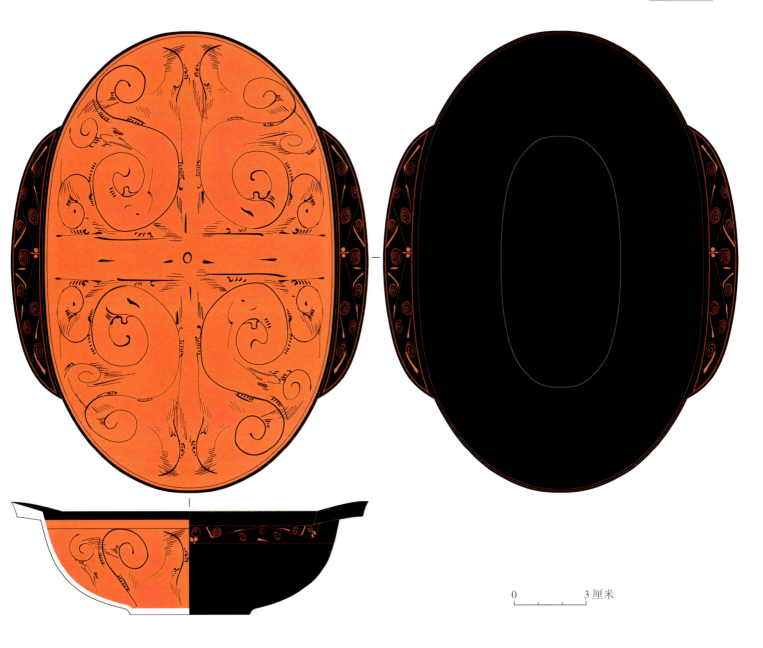

彩图七一　六区下层出土D型漆耳杯（M1Ⅵ：5022）

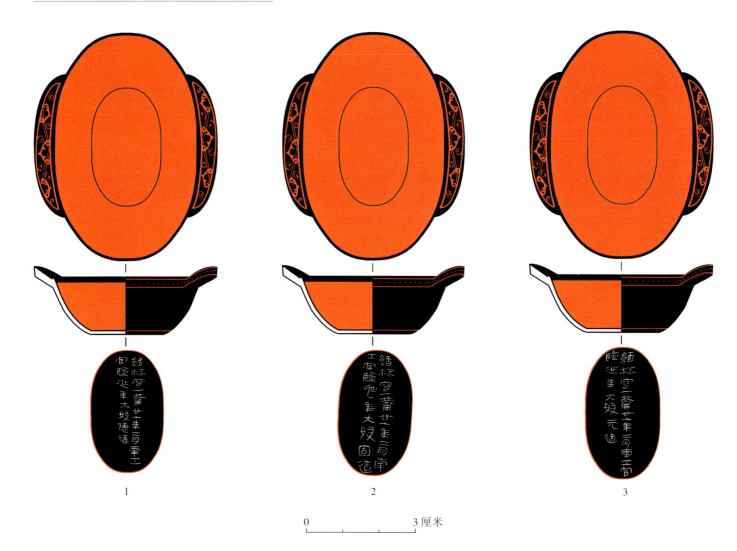

1   2   3

0   3 厘米

彩图七二   六区下层出土 E 型漆耳杯
1. M1Ⅵ：4628   2. M1Ⅵ：4653   3. M1Ⅵ：4630

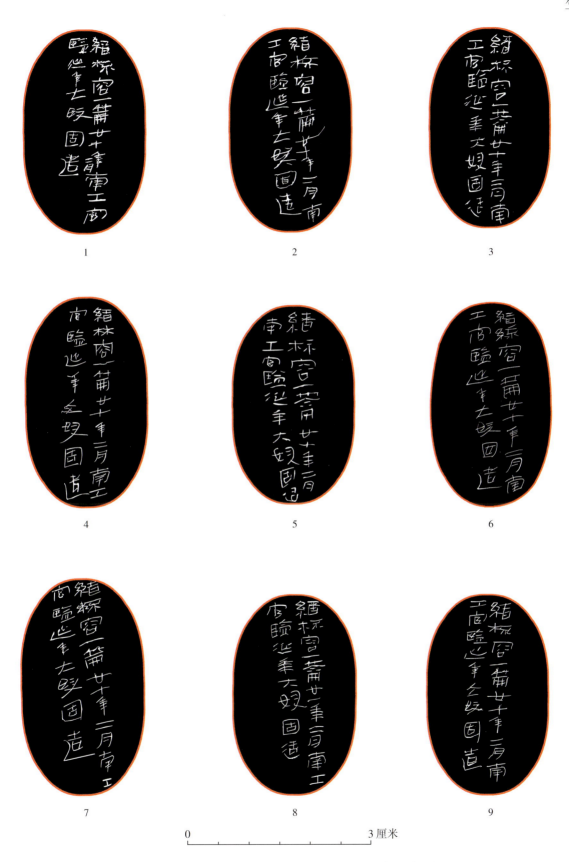

彩图七三　六区下层出土E型漆耳杯上的文字（放大）

1. M1Ⅵ：4629　2. M1Ⅵ：4632　3. M1Ⅵ：4636　4. M1Ⅵ：4642　5. M1Ⅵ：4643　6. M1Ⅵ：4645　7. M1Ⅵ：4654　8. M1Ⅵ：4657　9. M1Ⅵ：4658

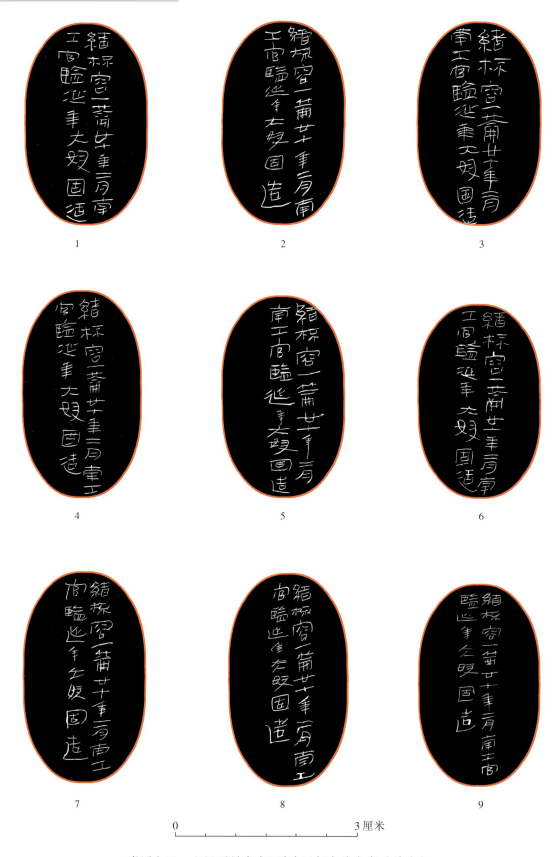

彩图七四　六区下层出土E型漆耳杯上的文字（放大）

1. M1Ⅵ：4659　2. M1Ⅵ：4660　3. M1Ⅵ：4661　4. M1Ⅵ：4663　5. M1Ⅵ：4666　6. M1Ⅵ：4669　7. M1Ⅵ：4671　8. M1Ⅵ：4673　9. M1Ⅵ：4674

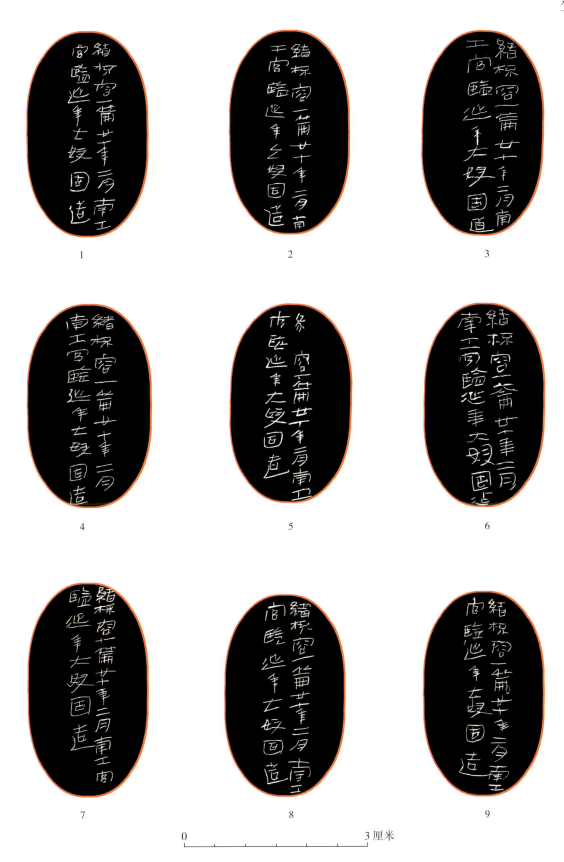

彩图七五　六区下层出土E型漆耳杯上的文字（放大）

1. M1Ⅵ：4683　2. M1Ⅵ：4689　3. M1Ⅵ：4690　4. M1Ⅵ：4694　5. M1Ⅵ：4795　6. M1Ⅵ：4701　7. M1Ⅵ：4878　8. M1Ⅵ：4880　9. M1Ⅵ：4881

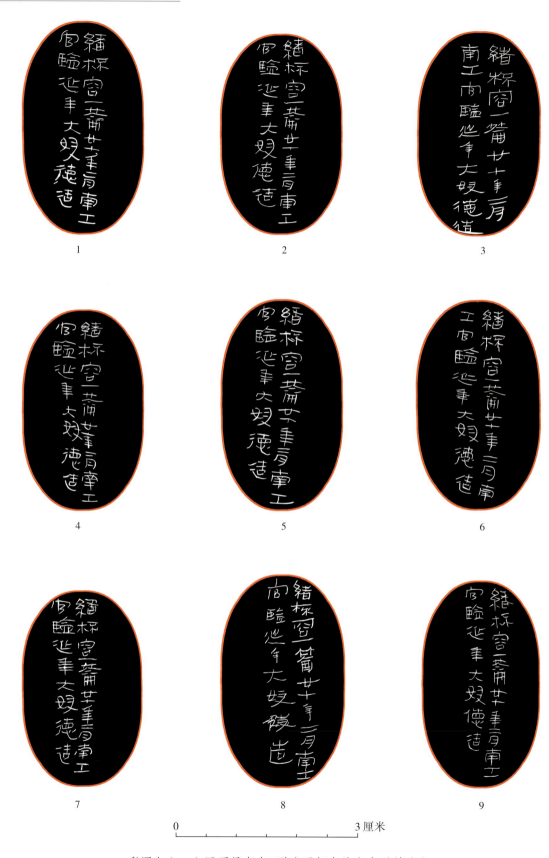

彩图七六　六区下层出土E型漆耳杯上的文字（放大）

1. M1Ⅵ：4635　2. M1Ⅵ：4637　3. M1Ⅵ：4638　4. M1Ⅵ：4640　5. M1Ⅵ：4648　6. M1Ⅵ：4651　7. M1Ⅵ：4665　8. M1Ⅵ：4667　9. M1Ⅵ：4670

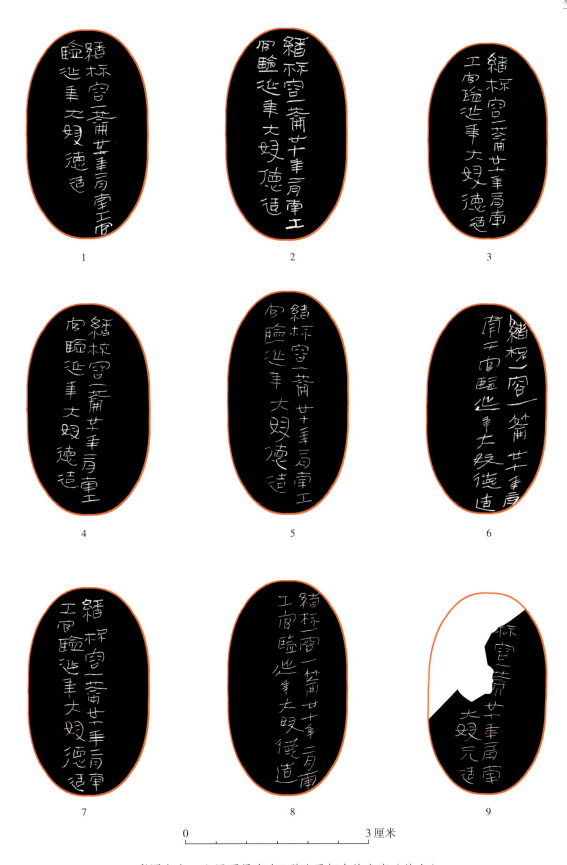

彩图七七　六区下层出土E型漆耳杯上的文字（放大）

1. M1Ⅵ：4684　2. M1Ⅵ：4685　3. M1Ⅵ：4686　4. M1Ⅵ：4687　5. M1Ⅵ：4692　6. M1Ⅵ：4702　7. M1Ⅵ：4882　8. M1Ⅵ：4883　9. M1Ⅵ：4884

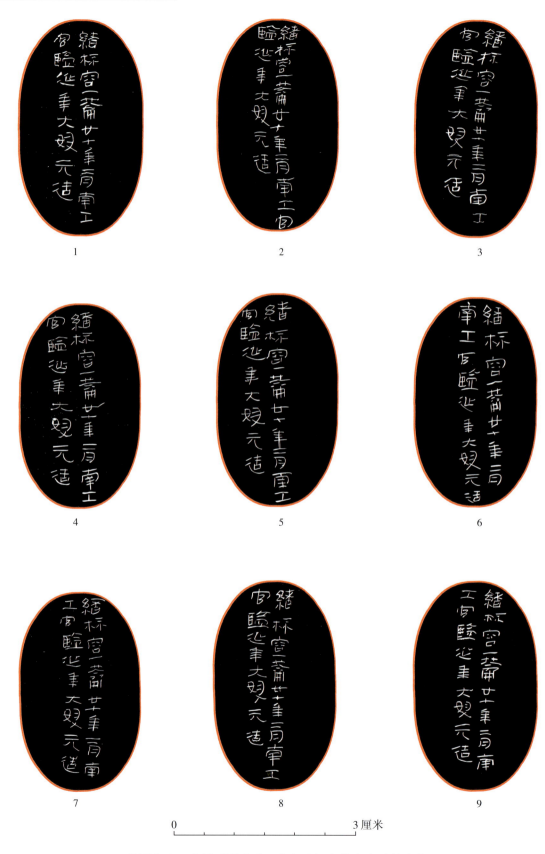

彩图七八　六区下层出土E型漆耳杯上的文字（放大）

1. M1Ⅵ：4631　2. M1Ⅵ：4632　3. M1Ⅵ：4634　4. M1Ⅵ：4639　5. M1Ⅵ：4641　6. M1Ⅵ：4644　7. M1Ⅵ：4649　8. M1Ⅵ：4650　9. M1Ⅵ：4652

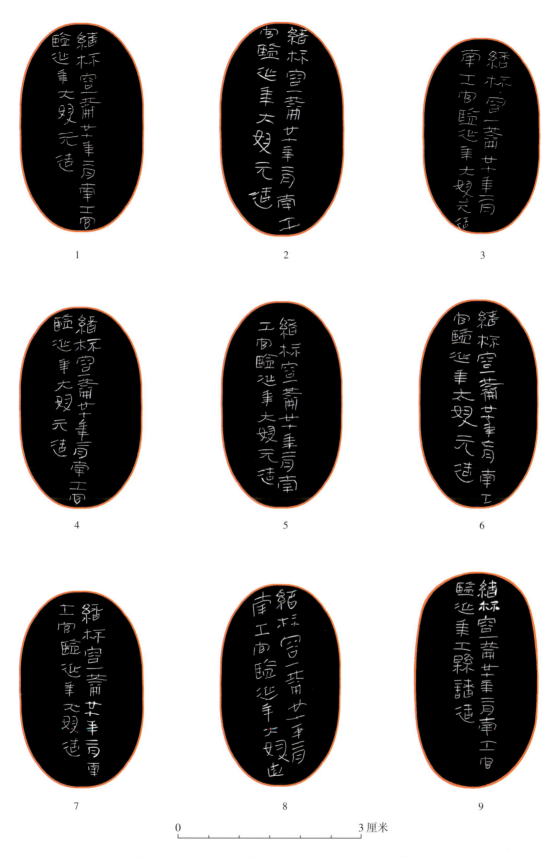

彩图七九　六区下层出土E型漆耳杯上的文字（放大）

1. M1Ⅵ：4662　2. M1Ⅵ：4664　3. M1Ⅵ：4672　4. M1Ⅵ：4680　5. M1Ⅵ：4688　6. M1Ⅵ：4697　7. M1Ⅵ：4656　8. M1Ⅵ：4879　9. M1Ⅵ：5057

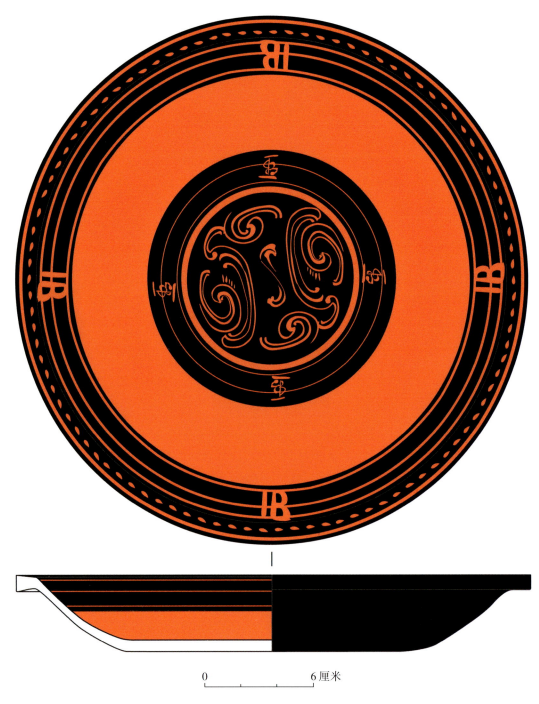

彩图八〇 六区下层出土B型漆盘（M1Ⅵ∶3844）

0 ⌐——————————⌐ 6厘米

彩图八一　六区下层出土B型漆盘（M1Ⅵ：4823）

彩图八二 六区下层出土B型漆盘（M1Ⅵ：4824）

0   6厘米

彩图八三　六区下层出土B型漆盘（M1Ⅵ：4825）

0   6厘米

彩图八四　六区下层出土B型漆盘（M1Ⅵ：4832）

0 _____ 3厘米

彩图八五 六区下层出土C型漆盘（M1Ⅵ：4723）

0 ⊢—⊢—⊢—⊢ 3厘米

彩图八六　六区下层出土C型漆盘（M1Ⅵ：4723）外底铭文

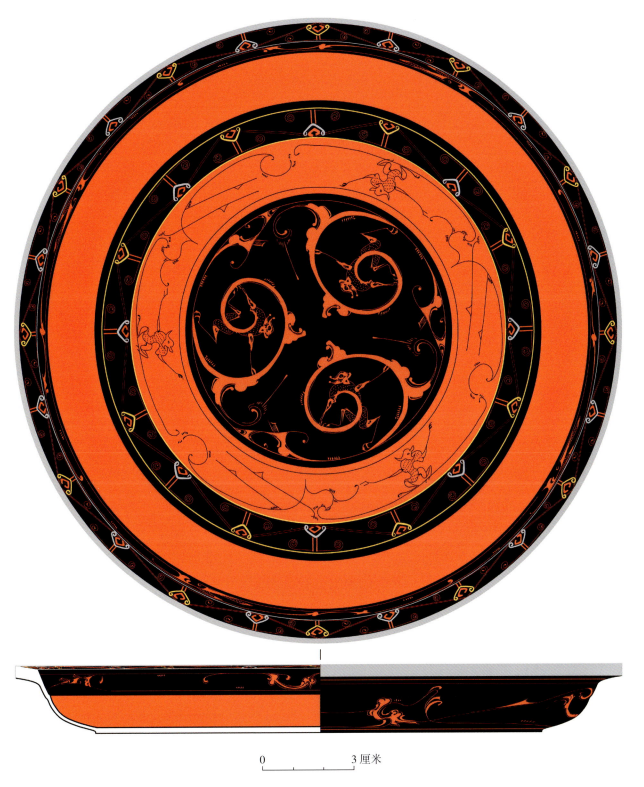

彩图八七　六区下层出土C型漆盘（M1Ⅵ：4724）

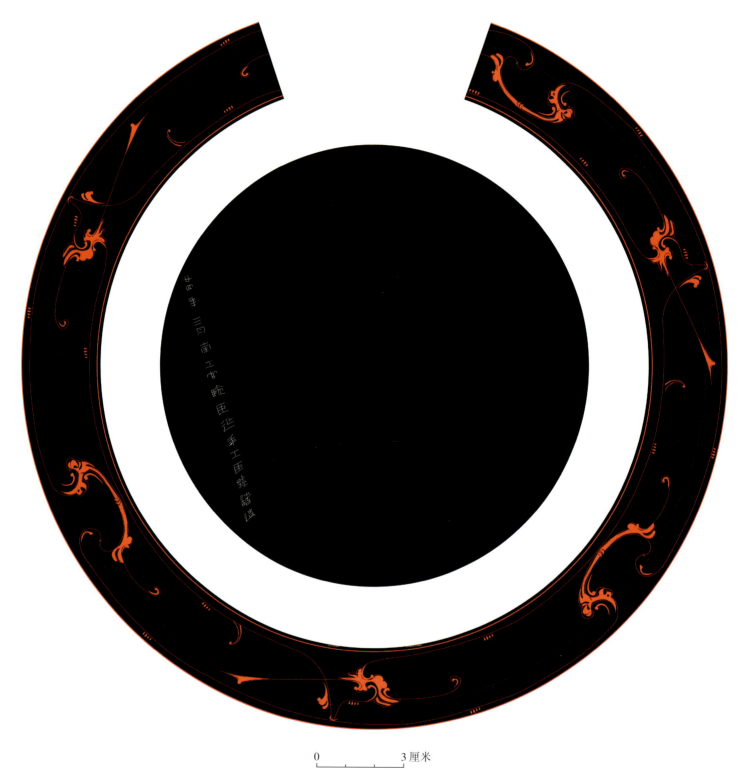

0 |———|———| 3厘米

彩图八八　六区下层出土C型漆盘（M1Ⅵ：4724）外底铭文

0 　　　　　　3厘米

彩图八九　六区下层出土C型漆盘（M1Ⅵ：4725）

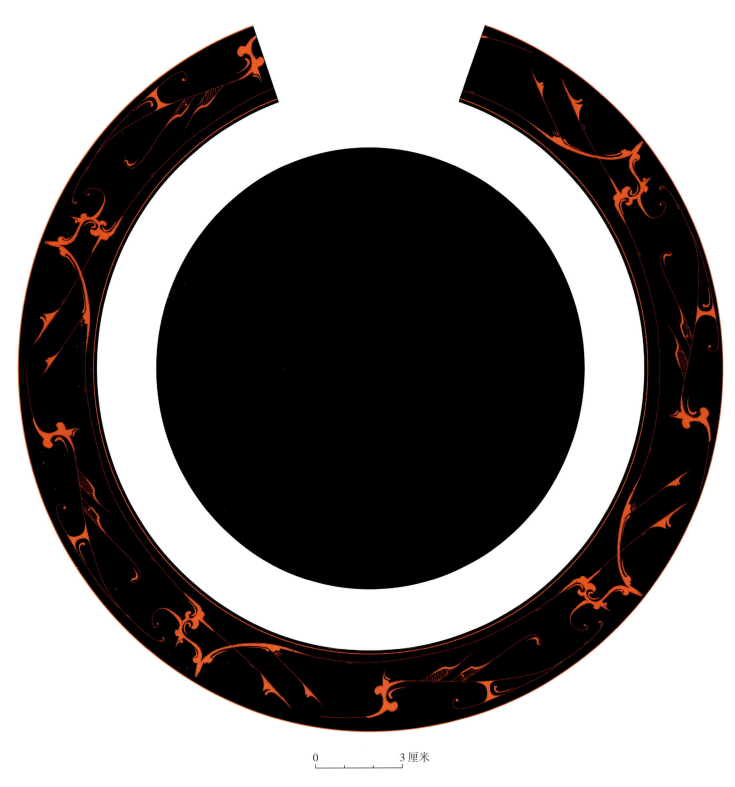

0   3 厘米

彩图九〇　六区下层出土C型漆盘外腹纹饰（M1Ⅵ：4725）

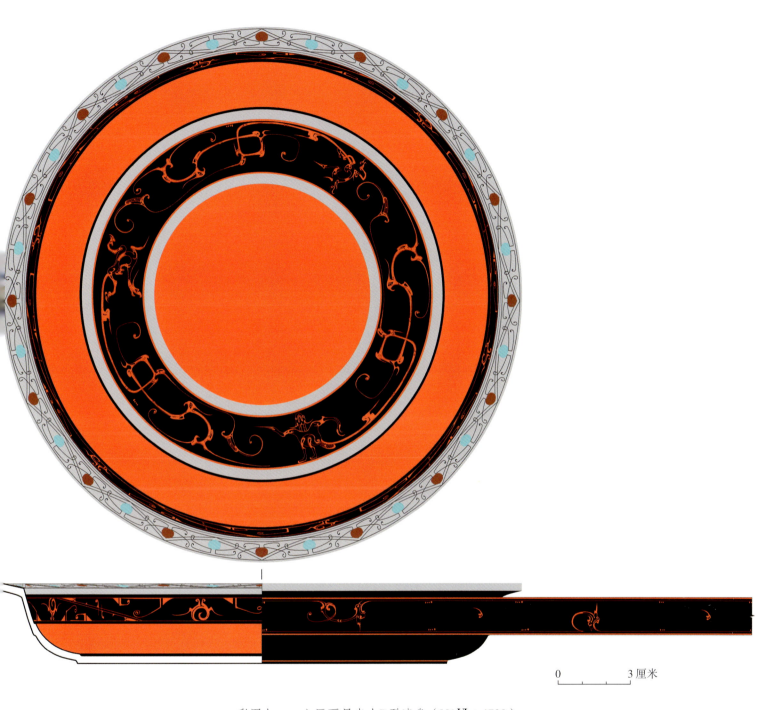

0   3厘米

彩图九一　六区下层出土D型漆盘（M1Ⅵ：4729）

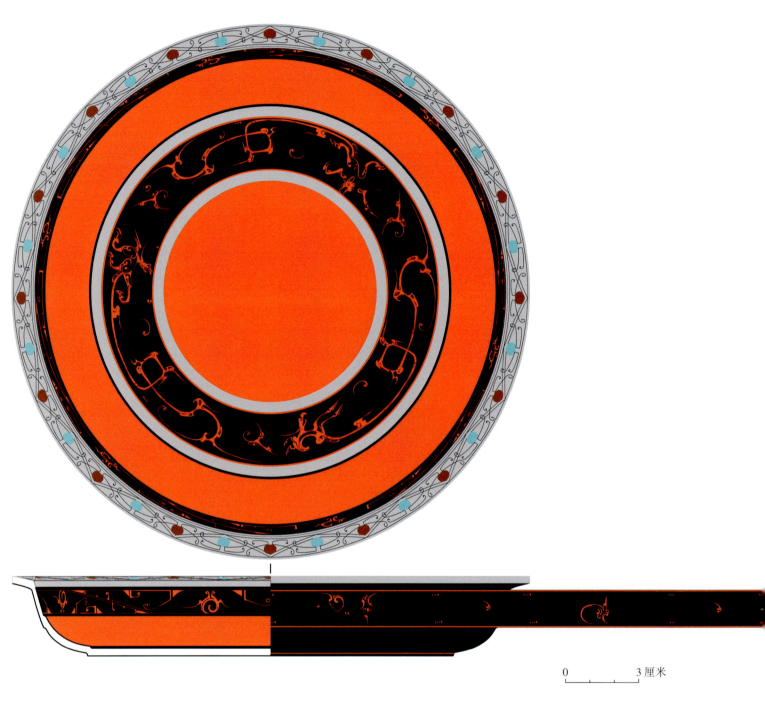

彩图九二 六区下层出土D型漆盘（M1Ⅵ：4732）

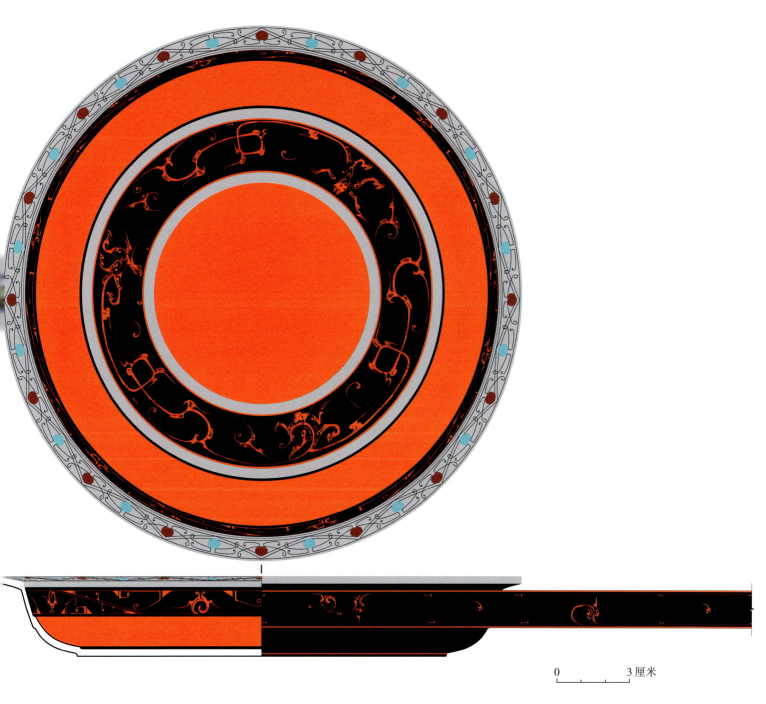

0 ⊢⊣⊢⊣ 3厘米

彩图九三　六区下层出土D型漆盘（M1Ⅵ：4733）

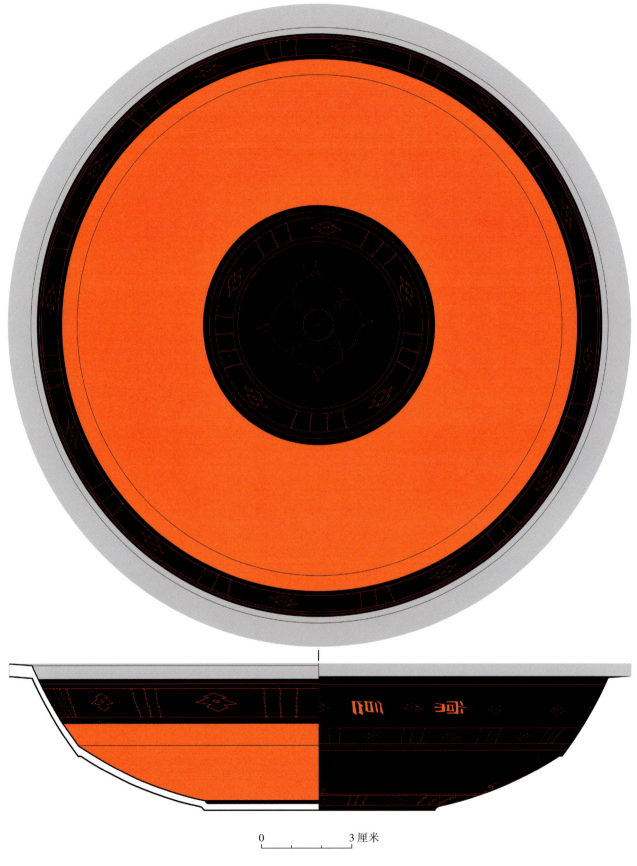

0 ⊢——————⊣ 3厘米

彩图九四　六区下层出土E型漆盘（M1Ⅵ：4728）

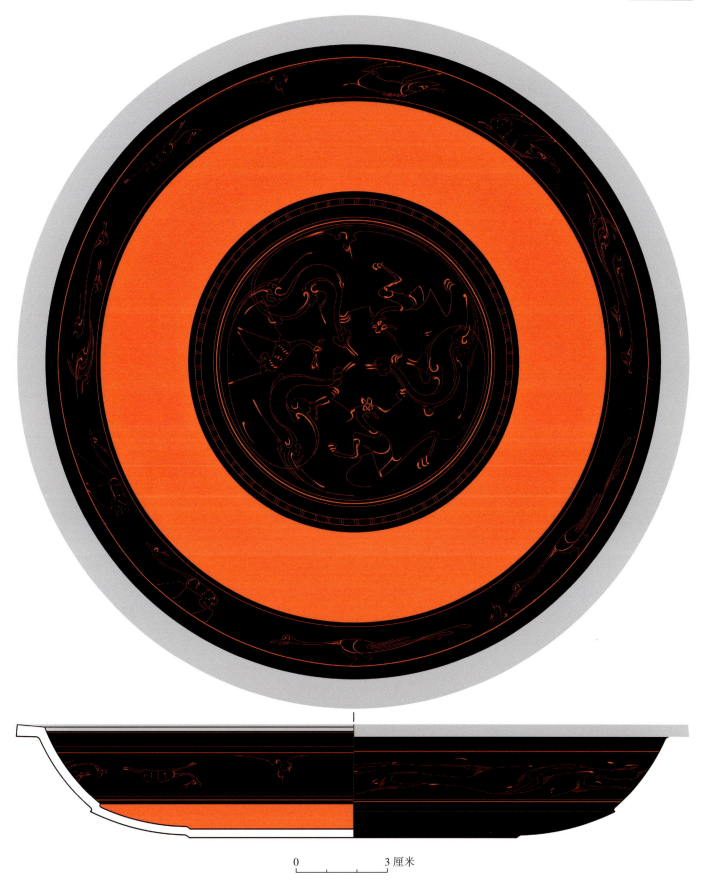

0　　　　　　　　3厘米

彩图九五　六区下层出土E型漆盘（M1Ⅵ：5063）

0   3厘米

彩图九六 　六区下层出土E型漆盘（M1Ⅵ：5065）

0 ⸺ 3厘米

彩图九七　六区下层出土E型漆盘（M1Ⅵ：5066）

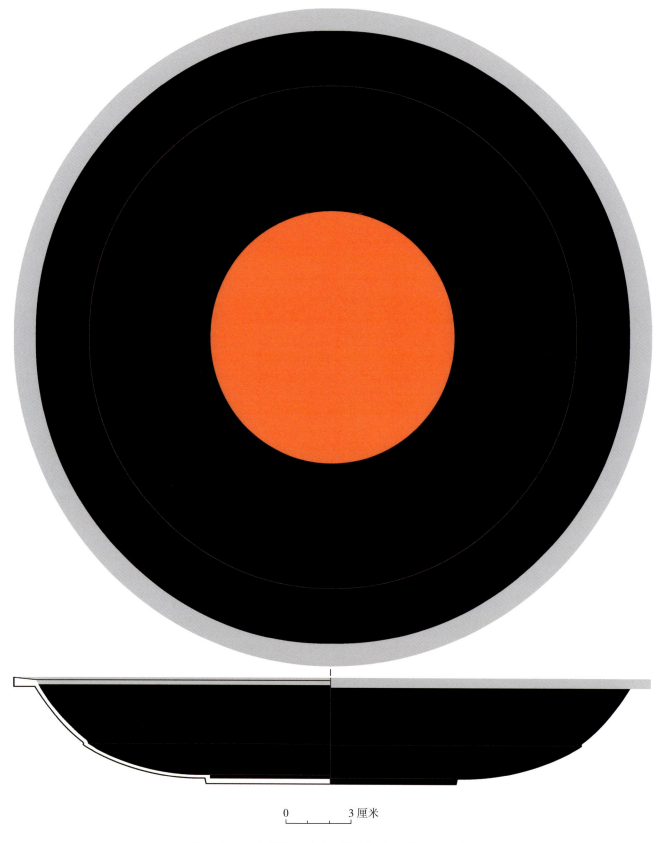

0 ⊢━━━┴━━━┤ 3厘米

彩图九八 六区下层出土E型漆盘（M1Ⅵ：5068）

1

2

0   6厘米

彩图九九　1号墓外棺残片
1. M1Ⅵ：4735　2. M1Ⅵ：4736

0   6 厘米

彩图一〇〇　六区下层出土G型漆盘（M1Ⅵ：3954）

0   12厘米

彩图一〇一　六区下层出土J型漆盘（M1Ⅵ：4413）

0   12 厘米

彩图一〇二　六区下层出土J型漆盘（M1Ⅵ：5639）

0 ——————— 6厘米

彩图一〇三　六区下层出土J型漆盘（M1Ⅵ：5640）

中常飤

彩图一〇四　六区下层出土J型漆盘（M1Ⅵ：5641）

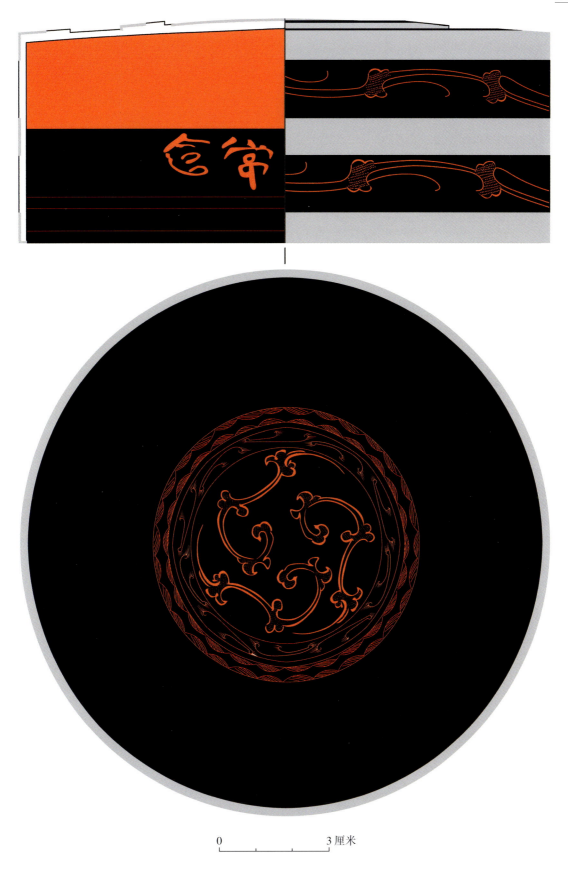

0   3厘米

彩图一○五　六区下层出土A型漆奁（M1Ⅵ：3894）奁盖剖视图及内底纹饰

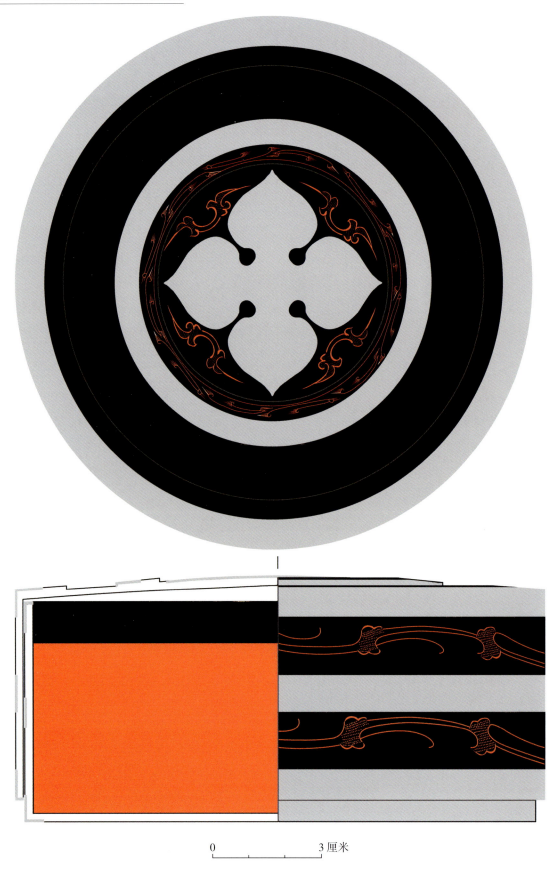

0   3厘米

彩图一〇六　六区下层出土A型漆奁（M1Ⅵ∶3894）奁盖俯视及奁剖视图

0   3厘米

彩图一〇七　六区下层出土A型漆奁（M1Ⅵ：3894）奁身内底纹饰及剖视图

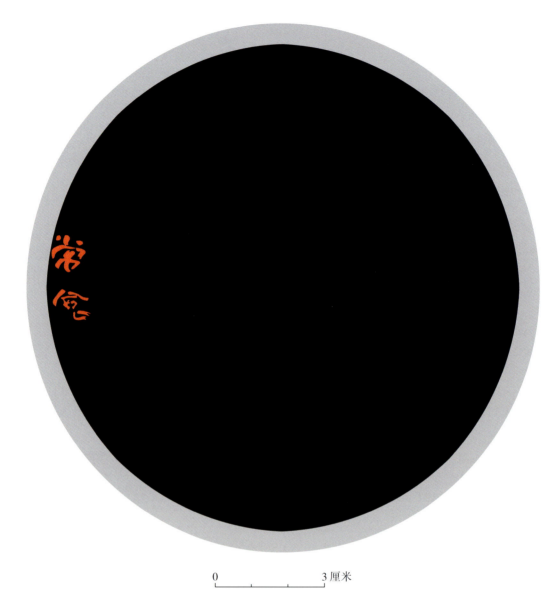

0   3厘米

彩图一〇八　六区下层出土A型漆奁（M1Ⅵ：3894）奁身外底铭文

彩图一〇九 六区下层出土B型漆奁（M1Ⅵ：4738）奁盖俯视、剖视图

1

2

0 ⊢———⊣ 6 厘米

彩图一一〇 六区下层出土 D 型漆奁（M1Ⅵ：3934）

1. 奁盖及外壁纹饰 　2. 奁身剖视图及外壁纹饰

0 —————————— 3厘米

彩图一一一 六区下层出土D型漆奁（M1Ⅵ：3934）奁身内底纹饰

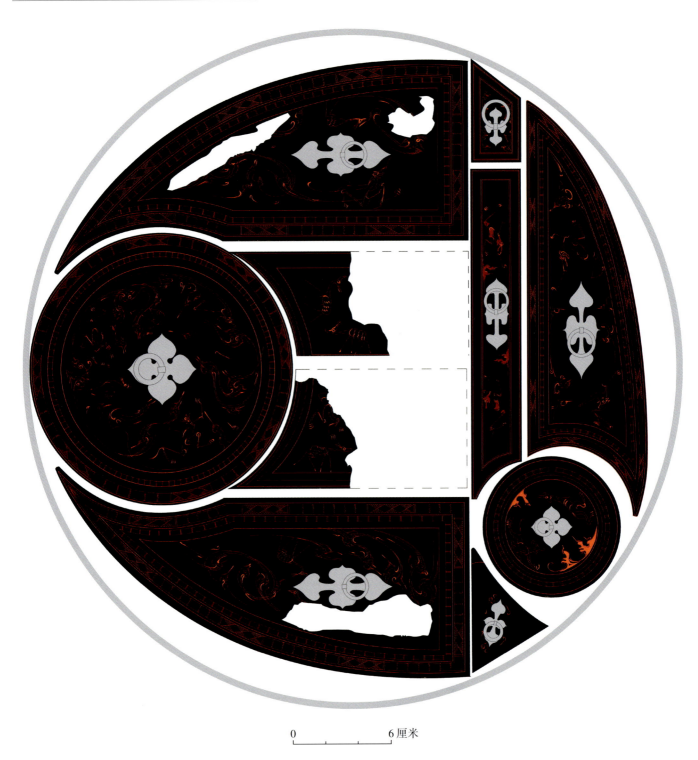

0   6 厘米

彩图一一二　六区下层出土D型漆奁（M1Ⅵ：3934）内子奁分布状况

0 _____ 3厘米

彩图一一三　六区下层出土D型漆奁内子奁（M1Ⅵ：3934-1）奁盖俯视图

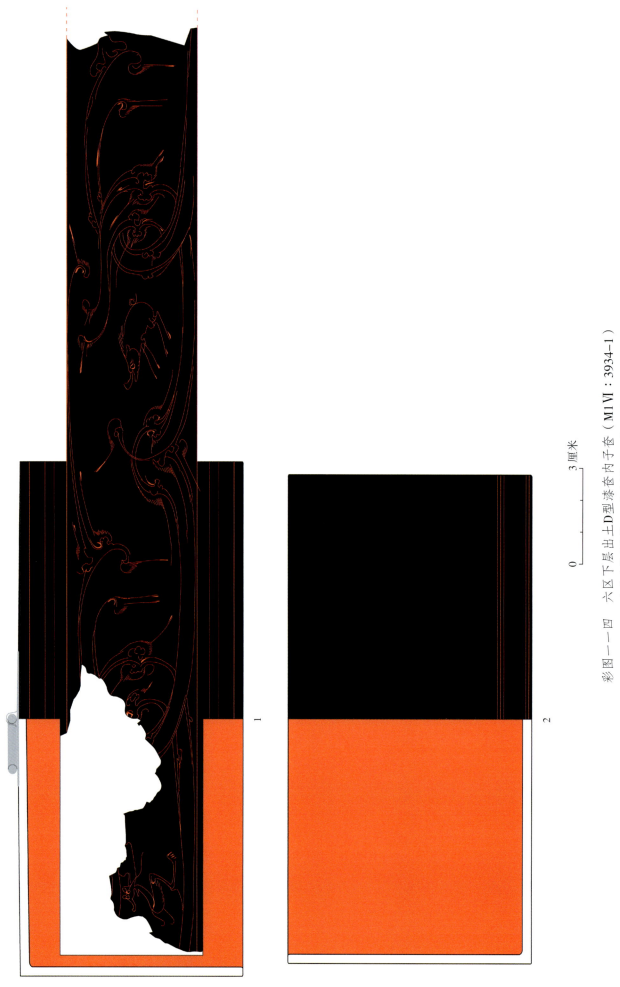

彩图一一四 六区下层出土D型漆奁内子奁（M1Ⅵ：3934-1）

1. 奁盖及外壁纹饰 2. 奁身剖视图及外壁纹饰

0   3 厘米

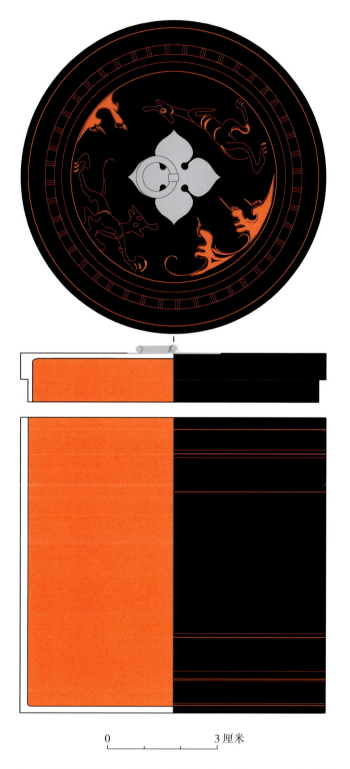

0   3厘米

彩图一一五　六区下层出土D型漆奁内子奁（M1Ⅵ：3934–2）俯视、剖视图

彩图一一六　六区下层出土 D 型漆奁子套内漆后视图

1. M1Ⅵ：3934-2-1　2. M1Ⅵ：3934-2-2

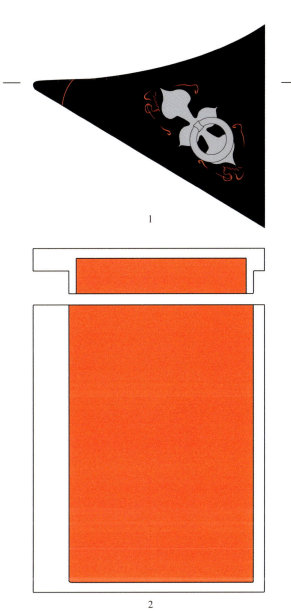

1

2

3

0   3厘米

彩图一一七　六区下层出土D型漆奁内子奁（M1Ⅵ：3934-3）

1.俯视外壁纹饰　2.剖视外壁纹饰　3.奁身外壁纹饰

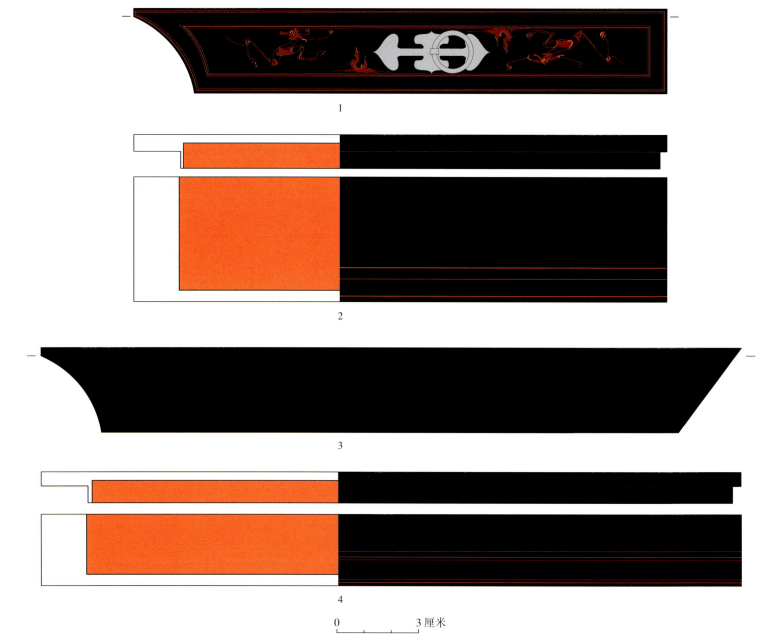

彩图一一八　六区下层出土D型漆奁内子奁俯视、剖视图

1、2. M1Ⅵ：3934-4　　3、4. M1Ⅵ：3934-6

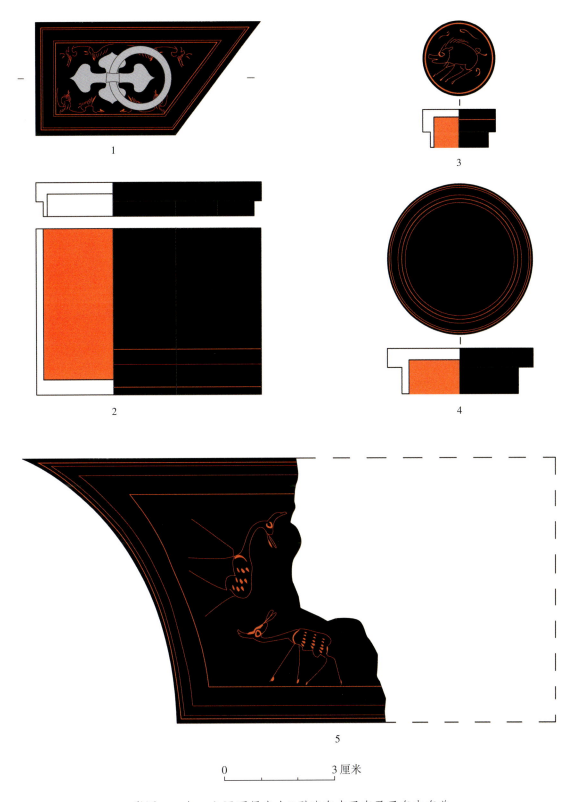

彩图一一九　六区下层出土D型漆奁内子奁及子奁内奁盖

1、2. M1Ⅵ：3934-5俯视、剖视图　3、4. M1Ⅵ：3934-9-1、M1Ⅵ：3934-9-2奁盖　5. M1Ⅵ：3934-9俯视图

彩图一二〇 六区下层出土 D 型漆奁内子奁（M1Ⅵ：3934-7）

1.俯视图 2.剖视图

1

2

0 _____ 3厘米

彩图一二一　六区下层出土D型漆奁内子奁（M1Ⅵ：3934-8）

1.俯视图　2.剖视图

0   3厘米

彩图一二二　六区下层出土D型漆奁内子奁（M1Ⅵ：3934-8）盖身外壁纹饰

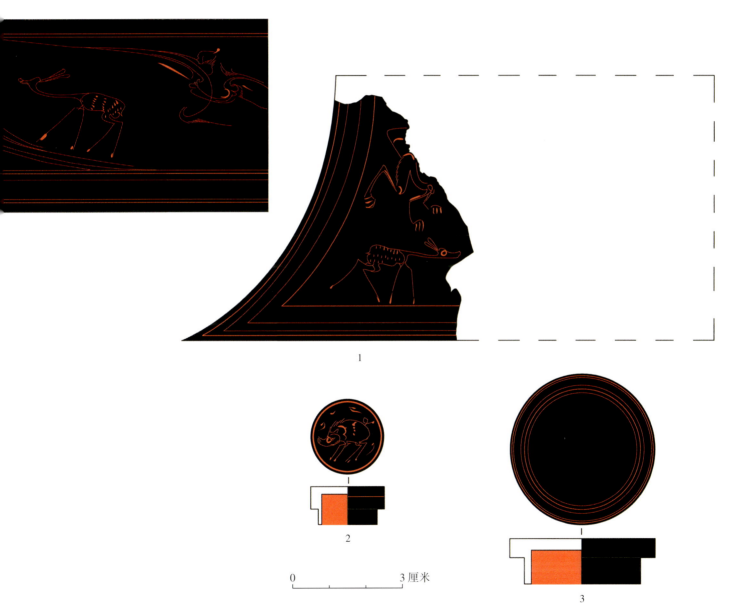

彩图一二三　六区下层出土D型漆奁内子奁及子奁内奁盖（M1Ⅵ：3934-10）

1. 俯视图　2、3.奁盖（M1Ⅵ：3934-10-1、M1Ⅵ：3934-10-2）

1

2

0　　　　　　3厘米

彩图一二四　六区下层出土D型漆奁内子奁（M1Ⅵ：3934–11）
1. 俯视图　2. 剖视图

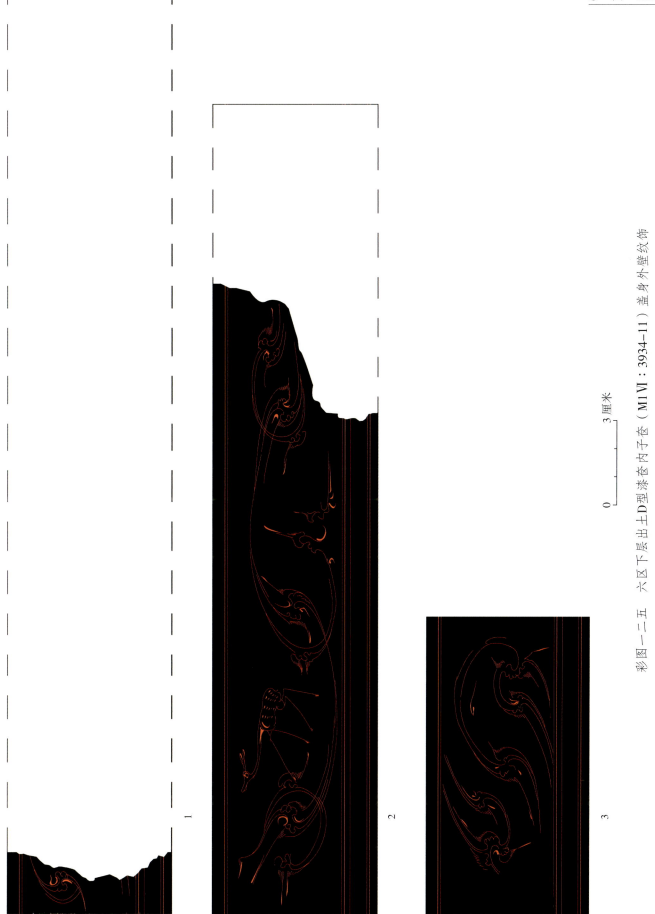

0 3 厘米

彩图一二五　六区下层出土D型漆奁内子奁（M1Ⅵ：3934-11）盖身外壁纹饰

0   3厘米

彩图一二六 六区下层出土B型漆卮（M1Ⅵ∶3910-1）盖俯视图

0 —— 3 厘米

彩图一二七 六区下层出土B型漆卮（M1Ⅵ：3910–1）剖视图

0   3厘米

彩图一二八　六区下层出土B型漆卮（M1Ⅵ：3910-2）盖俯视图

0 ___ 3 厘米

彩图一二九 六区下层出土B型漆卮（M1Ⅵ：3910-2）剖视图

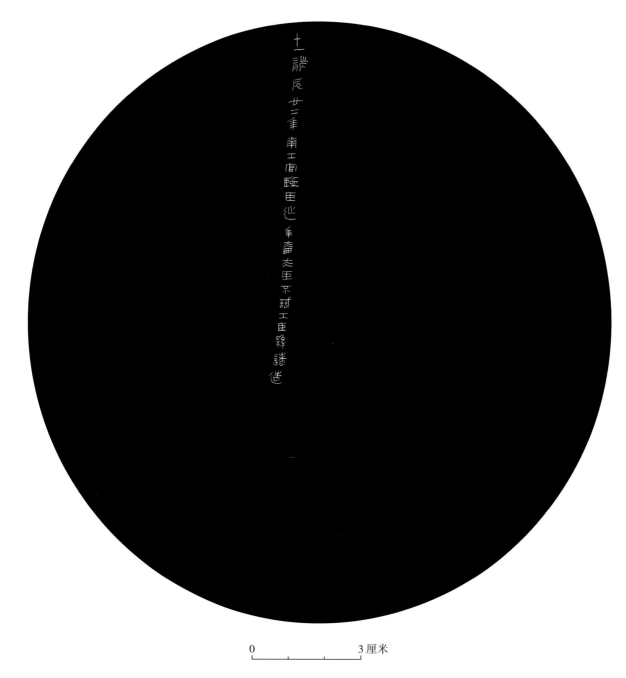

0   3厘米

彩图一三〇　六区下层出土B型漆卮（M1Ⅵ：3910-2）外底铭文

0 —————————— 3厘米

彩图一三一　六区下层出土B型漆卮（M1Ⅵ：3910–3）盖俯视图

彩图一三二　六区下层出土B型漆卮（M1Ⅵ∶3910-3）剖视图

0 ⌞____⌟ 3 厘米

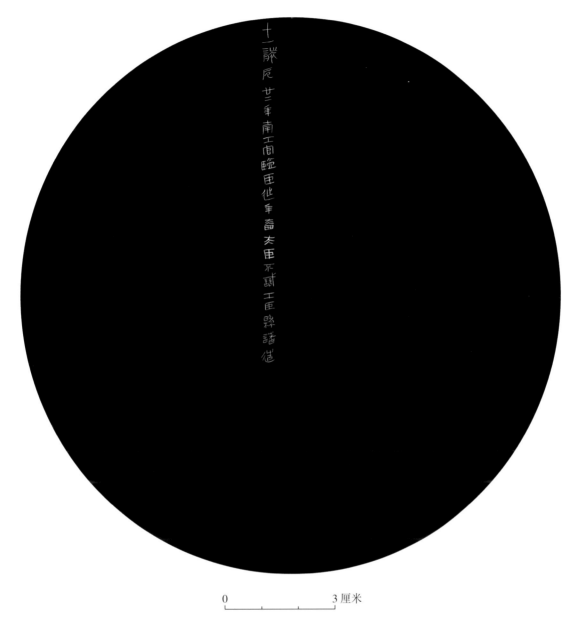

0   3厘米

彩图一三三　　六区下层出土B型漆卮（M1Ⅵ：3910-3）外底铭文

0   3 厘米

彩图一三四　六区下层出土 B 型漆卮（M1Ⅵ：3910-4）盖俯视图

彩图一三五 六区下层出土B型漆卮（M1Ⅵ：3910-4）剖视图

0 3厘米

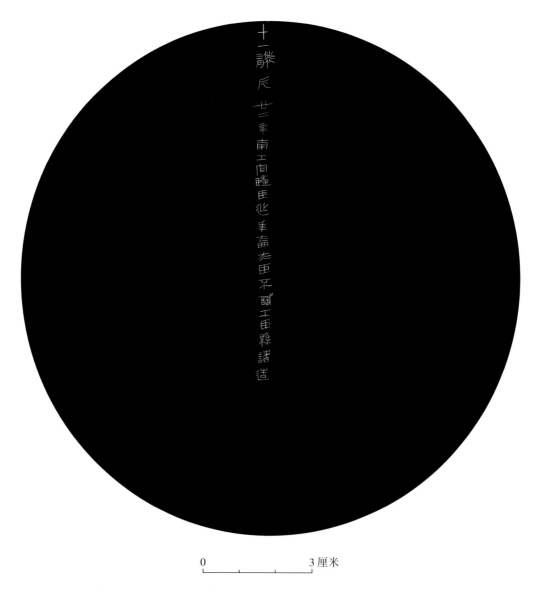

0 ⸺⸺⸺⸺ 3厘米

彩图一三六　六区下层出土B型漆卮（M1Ⅵ：3910–4）外底铭文

0 _____ 3厘米

彩图一三七　六区下层出土B型漆卮（M1Ⅵ：3912-1）盖俯视图

彩图一三八 六区下层出土B型漆卮（M1Ⅵ：3912-1）剖视图

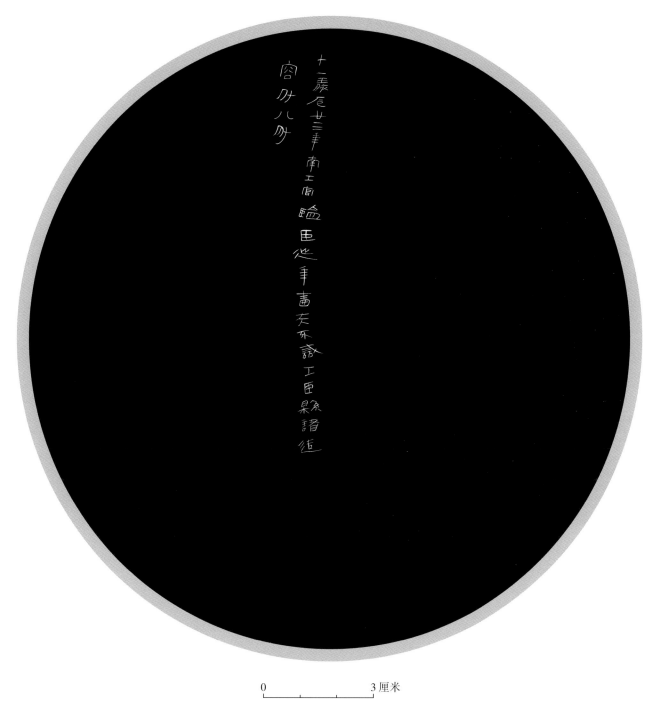

彩图一三九　六区下层出土 B 型漆卮（M1Ⅵ：3912-1）外底铭文

0   3 厘米

彩图一四〇　六区下层出土 B 型漆卮（M1Ⅵ：3912–2）盖俯视图

0 ____ 3 厘米

彩图一四一　六区下层出土B型漆巵（M1VI：3912-2）剖视图

0 _____ 3厘米

彩图一四二　六区下层出土 B 型漆卮（M1Ⅵ：3912-2）外底铭文

0 ⊢————————⊣ 3厘米

彩图一四三　六区下层出土B型漆卮（M1Ⅵ：3912-3）盖俯视图

0 ———— 3 厘米

彩图一四四　六区下层出土B型漆卮（M1Ⅵ：3912-3）剖视图

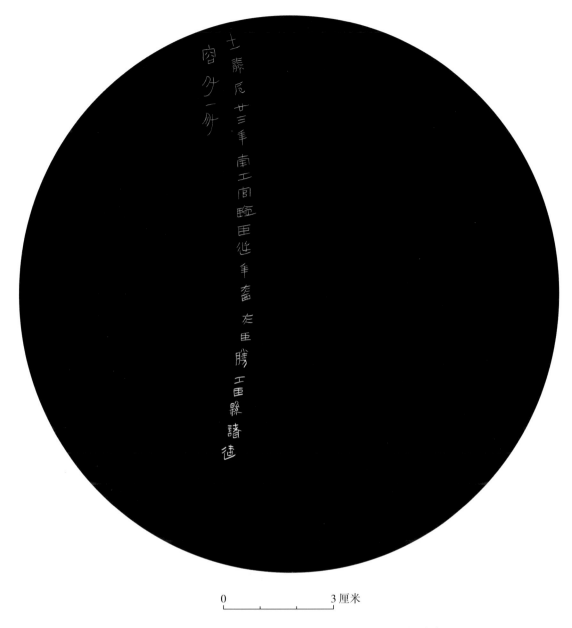

0   3厘米

彩图一四五　六区下层出土B型漆卮（M1Ⅵ：3912–3）外底铭文

0 ⊢——⊣——⊣ 3 厘米

彩图一四六　六区下层出土B型漆卮（M1Ⅵ：3912-4）盖俯视图

彩图一四七　六区下层出土B型漆卮（M1Ⅵ∶3912-4）剖视图

0 ⌞___⌟ 3厘米

0   3厘米

彩图一四八　六区下层出土B型漆卮（M1Ⅵ∶3912-4）外底铭文

0   3厘米

彩图一四九 六区下层出土B型漆卮（M1Ⅵ：3912-5）盖俯视图

彩图一五〇　六区下层出土B型漆卮（M1Ⅵ：3912-5）剖视图

0　　　　3厘米

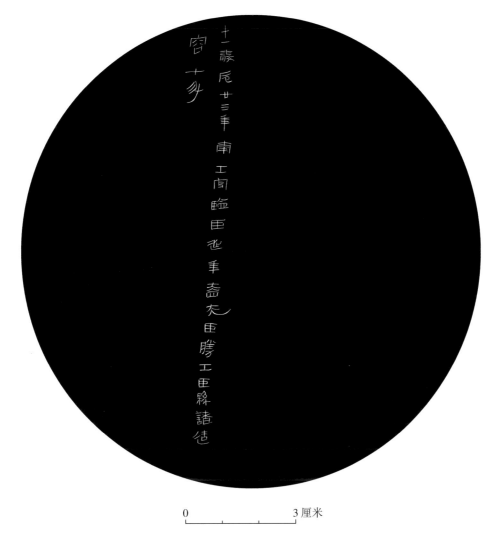

0 |———|———| 3厘米

彩图一五一　六区下层出土B型漆卮（M1Ⅵ：3912–5）外底铭文

1

2

彩图一五二　六区下层出土B型漆卮（M1Ⅵ：3912-6）

1.盖俯视图　2.外底铭文

0 3 厘米

彩图一五三 六区下层出土B型漆卮（M1Ⅵ：3912-6）剖视图

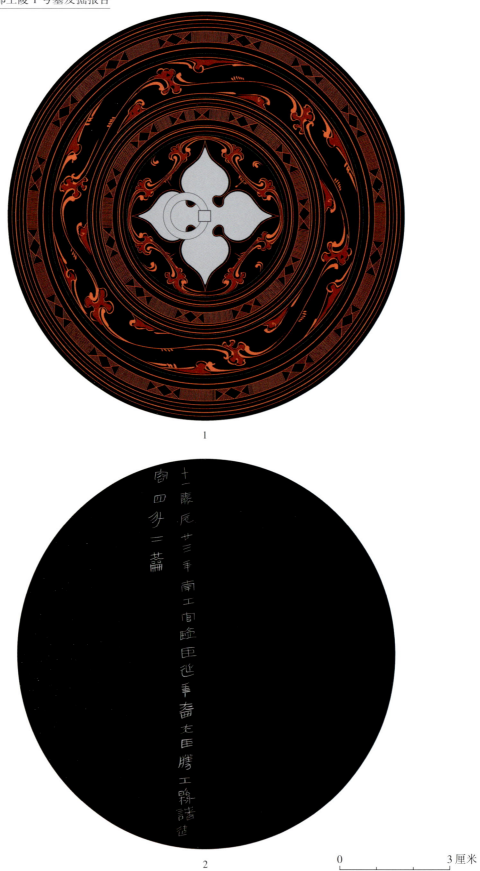

1

2

0   3 厘米

彩图一五四　六区下层出土B型漆卮（M1Ⅵ：3912-7）

1. 盖俯视图　2. 外底铭文

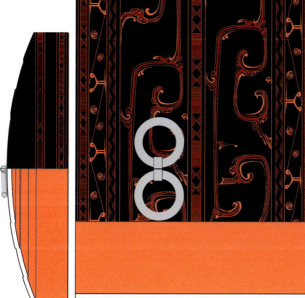

0   3 厘米

彩图一五五　六区下层出土B型漆卮（M1Ⅵ：3912-7）剖视图

1

2

0 ⊢─────────────┤ 3厘米

彩图一五六　六区下层出土B型漆卮（M1Ⅵ：3912-8）

1.盖俯视图　2.外底铭文

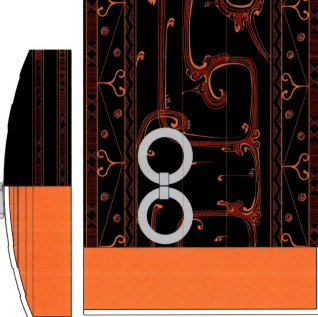

0 3厘米

彩图一五七 六区下层出土B型漆卮（M1Ⅵ：3912-8）剖视图

1

2

0   3 厘米

彩图一五八　六区下层出土B型漆卮（M1Ⅵ∶3912-9）

1. 盖俯视图　2. 外底铭文

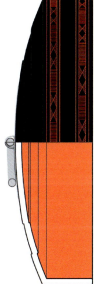

彩图一五九 六区下层出土B型漆卮（M1Ⅵ：3912-9）剖视图

0   3厘米

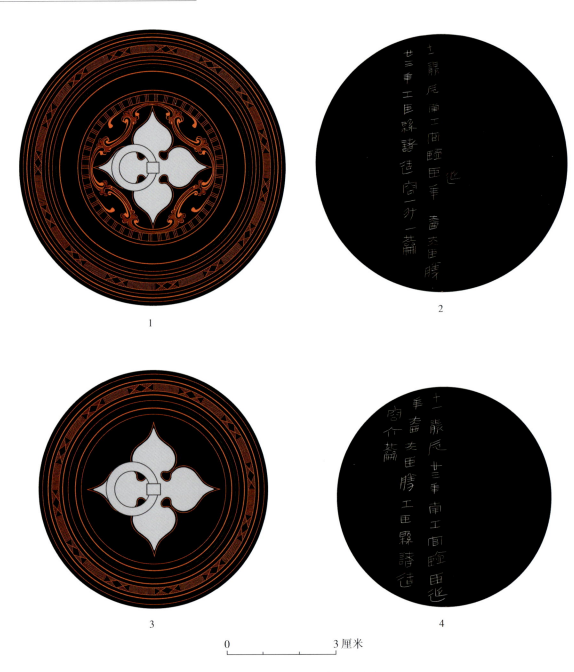

1

2

3

4

0   3厘米

彩图一六〇　六区下层出土B型漆卮

1、2.盖俯视图、外底铭文（M1Ⅵ：3912–10）　　3、4.盖俯视图、外底铭文（M1Ⅵ：3912–11）

彩图一六一 六区下层出土B型漆卮后剖视图

1. M1Ⅵ：3912-10 2. M1Ⅵ：3912-11

1

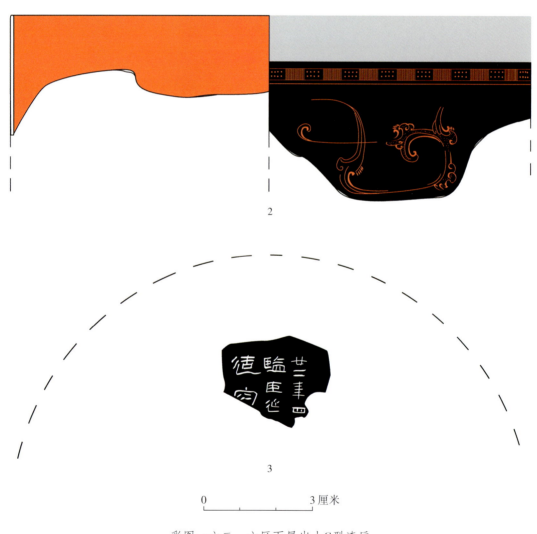

2

3

0　　　　　　　　3厘米

彩图一六二　六区下层出土 C 型漆厄

1. 外底铭文（M1Ⅵ：3826）　2、3. 剖视图、外底铭文（M1Ⅵ：3908）

0　　　　　　　　3厘米

彩图一六三　六区下层出土C型漆卮（M1Ⅵ：3908）盖俯视、剖视图

0   6 厘米

彩图一六四　六区下层出土漆樽（M1Ⅵ：3902）俯视图

0 ⊢—————┤ 6厘米

彩图一六五 六区下层出土漆樽（M1Ⅵ：3902）剖视图

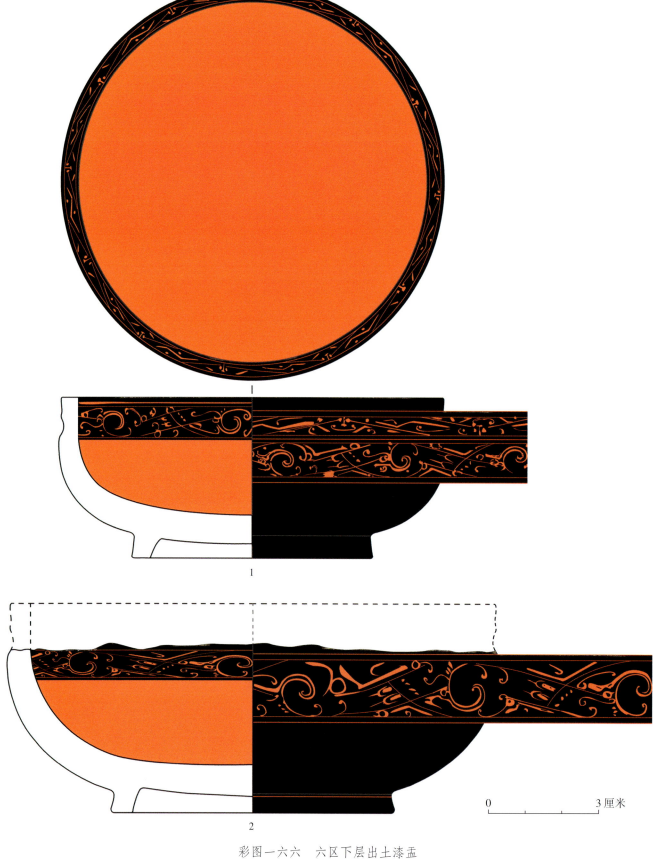

1

2

0 ————————— 3 厘米

彩图一六六　六区下层出土漆盂

1. M1Ⅵ：3901俯视、剖视图　2. M1Ⅵ：5845剖视图

彩图一六七　六区下层出土漆匜（M1Ⅵ：5070）俯视、剖视图

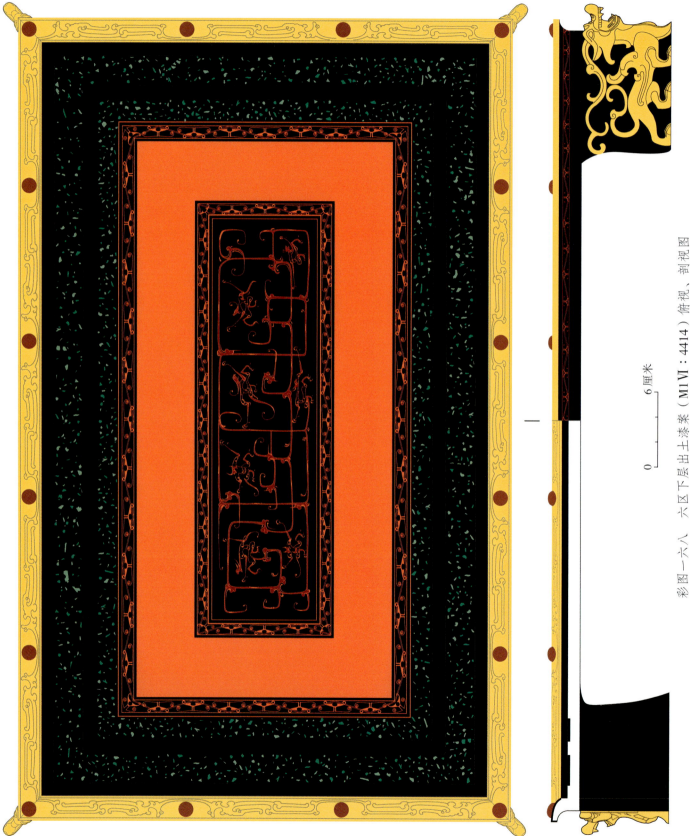

彩图一六八 六区下层出土漆案（M1VI∶4414）俯视、剖视图

0   6 厘米

彩图一六九　六区下层出土漆笥

1

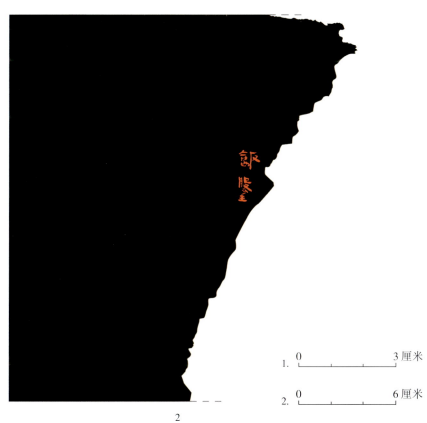

2

1. 0 ————— 3 厘米

2. 0 ————— 6 厘米

彩图一六九　六区下层出土漆笥

1. M1Ⅵ：3839　2. M1Ⅵ：4978

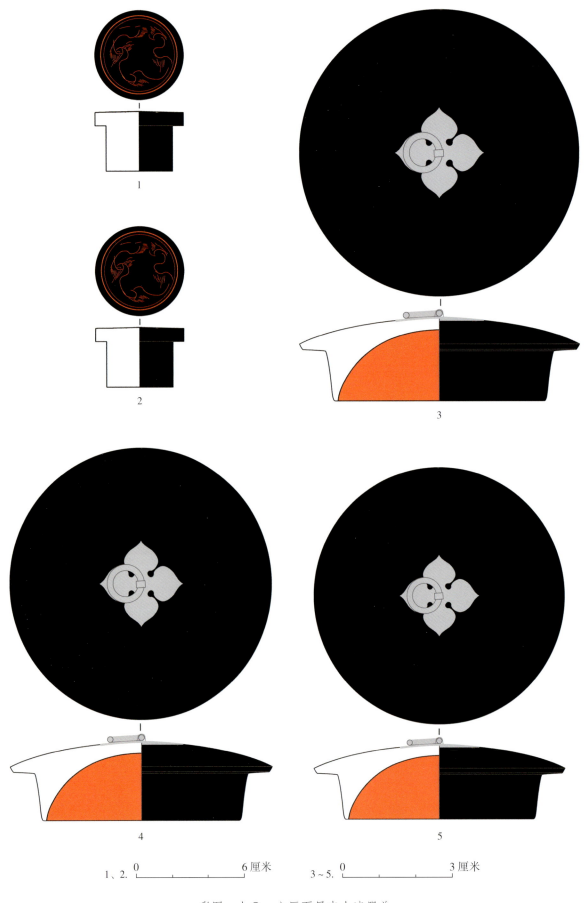

彩图一七〇　六区下层出土漆器盖

1. M1Ⅵ∶3840　2. M1Ⅵ∶3841　3. M1Ⅵ∶3891　4. M1Ⅵ∶3892　5. M1Ⅵ∶3893

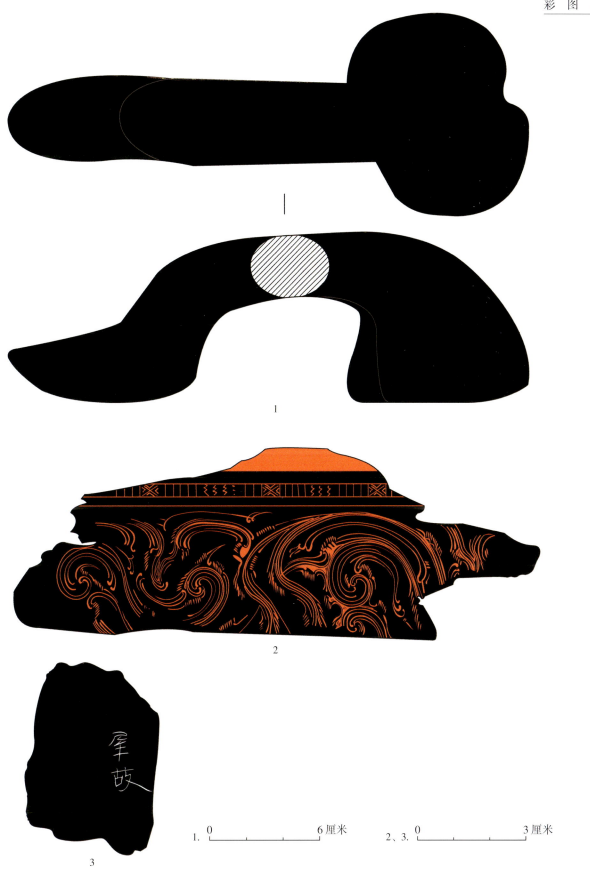

1

2

3

1. ├─────────┤ 0   6厘米   2、3. ├─────────┤ 0   3厘米

彩图一七一　六区下层出土漆器
1. M1Ⅵ：3810　2. M1Ⅵ：5016　3. M1Ⅵ：5058

彩图一七二 七A区下层出土A型漆耳杯（M1ⅦA：5018）

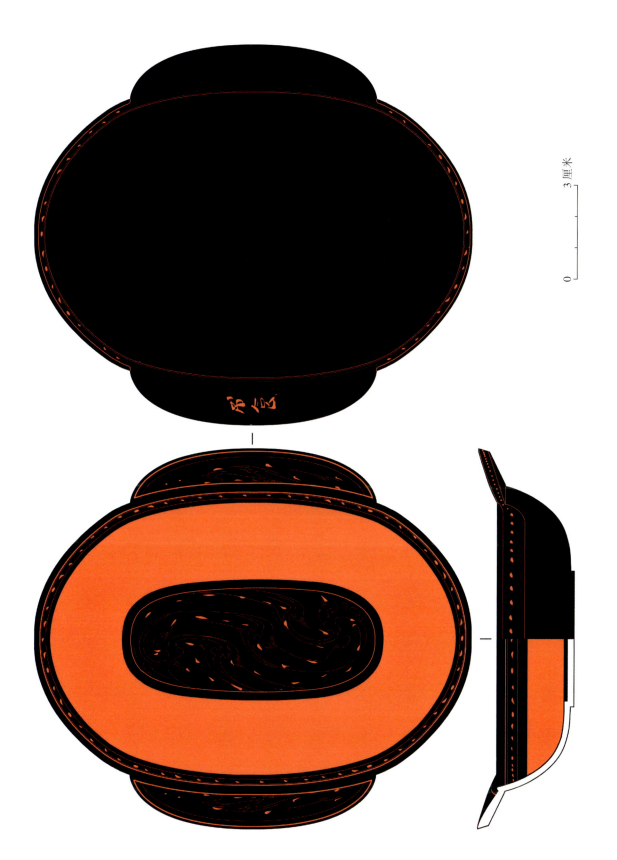

0　　　　3厘米

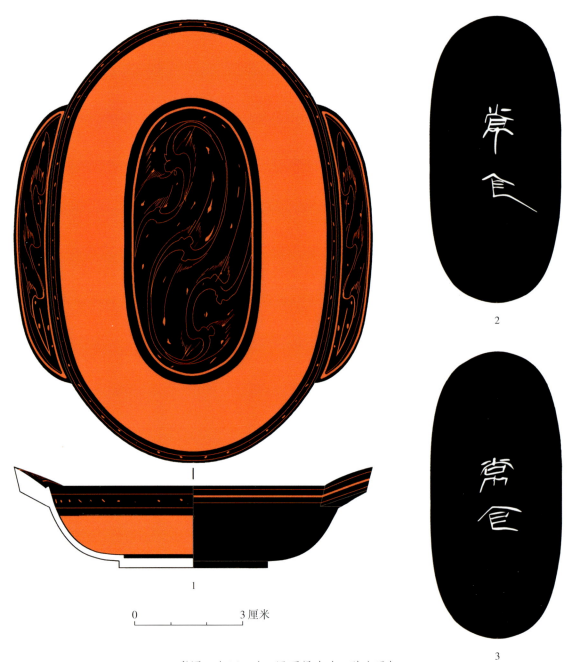

0　　　　　　　3厘米

彩图一七四　七A区下层出土A型漆耳杯

1. M1ⅦA：4979　　2. M1ⅦA：4986外底铭文　　3. M1ⅦA：4987外底铭文

0   3厘米

彩图一七五　七A区下层出土A型漆耳杯（M1ⅦA：5020）

0   3厘米

彩图一七六　七A区下层出土A型漆耳杯（M1ⅦA：5021）

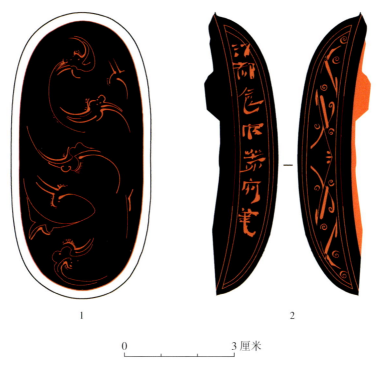

1

2

0 ⊢———————⊣ 3厘米

彩图一七七 七A区下层出土A型漆耳杯

1. M1ⅦA∶4981 2. M1ⅦA∶4982

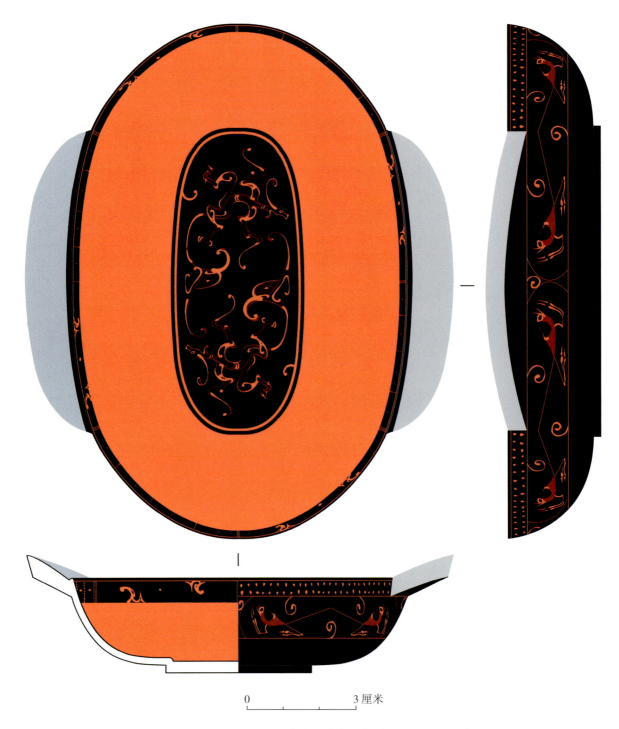

0   3 厘米

彩图一七八　七A区下层出土B型漆耳杯（M1ⅦA：5017）

彩图一七九　七A区下层出土漆奁（M1ⅦA：3903）

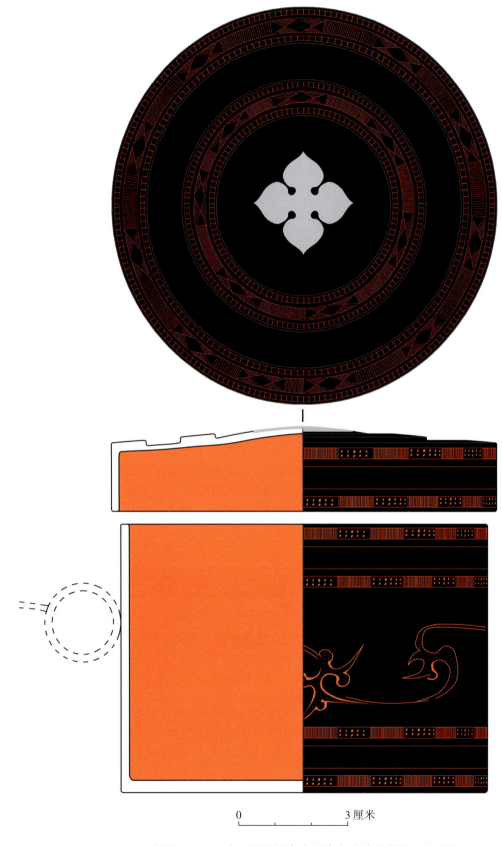

0   3厘米

彩图一八〇　七A区下层出土A型漆卮（M1ⅦA：4965）

彩图一八一　七A区下层出土A型漆卮（M1ⅦA：4984）

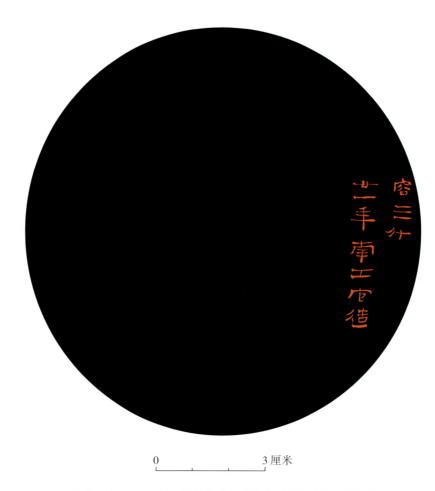

0   3 厘米

彩图一八二　七A区下层出土C型漆卮（M1ⅦA：4973）

彩图一八三　七A区下层出土漆樽（M1ⅦA：3911）

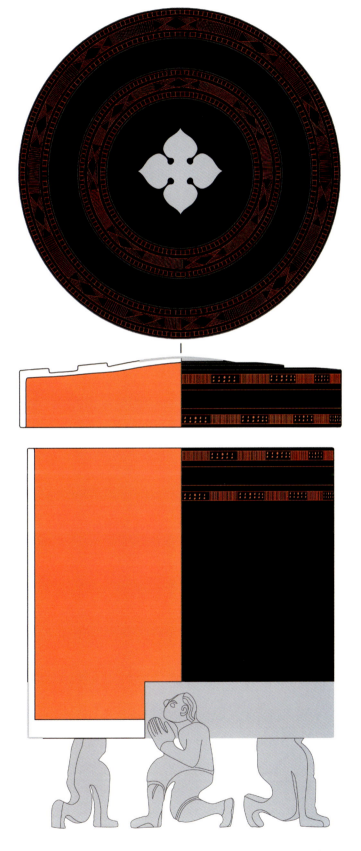

0 ⊢─────────┤ 3厘米

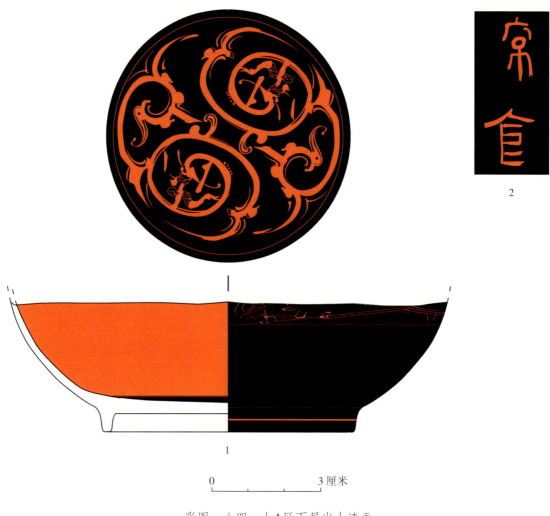

2

1

0   3厘米

彩图一八四　七A区下层出土漆盂

1. M1ⅦA：4967　2. M1ⅦA：4966

彩图一八五　七A区下层出土漆匜（M1ⅦA：5069）

0　　　　　6厘米

0 　　　　　6厘米

彩图一八六　七A区下层出土漆匜（M1ⅦA：3811）

0   6厘米

彩图一八七　七A区下层出土漆匜（M1ⅦA：3809）

0   6 厘米

彩图一八八 七A区下层出土漆匜（M1ⅦA：5047）

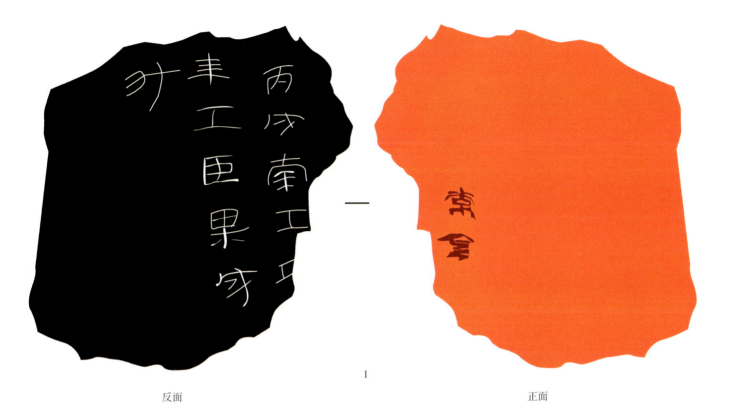

反面   1   正面

2

0   3 厘米

彩图一八九　七 A 区下层出土漆器
1. M1ⅦA：3817　2. M1ⅦA：4988

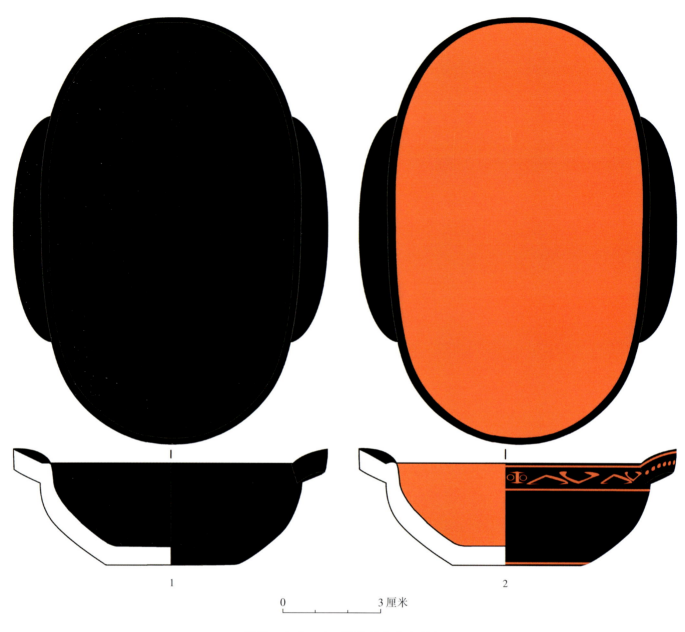

彩图一九〇　七 B 区下层出土漆耳杯
1. C 型（M1ⅦB：4182）　2. D 型（M1ⅦB：4338）

0   6厘米

彩图一九一　七B区下层出土B型漆盘（M1ⅦB：4183）

0   3厘米

彩图一九二　八区下层出土D型漆耳杯（M1Ⅷ：4248）

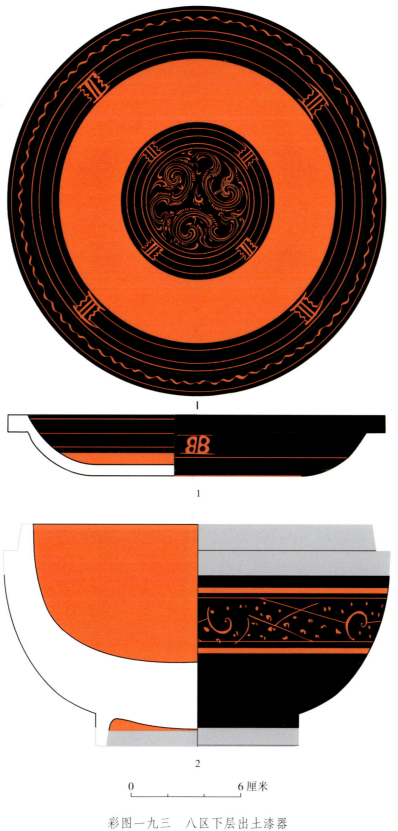

1

2

0   6厘米

彩图一九三　八区下层出土漆器
1. B型盘（M1Ⅷ：4231）　2. 盛（M1Ⅷ：4247）

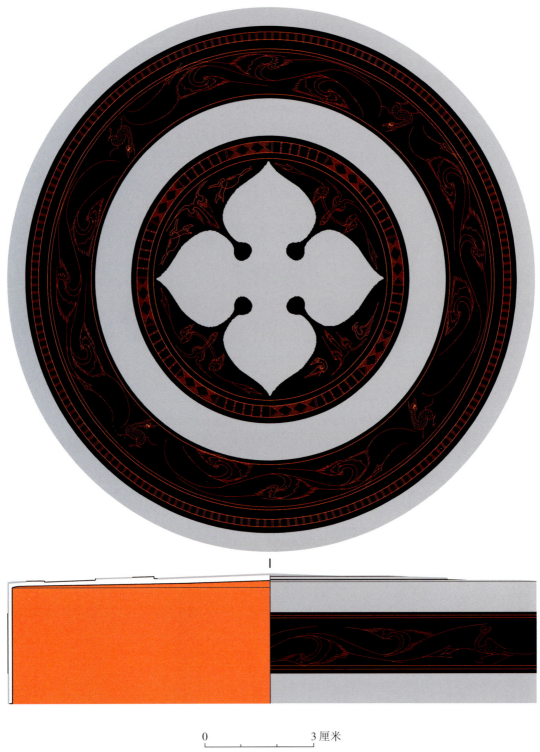

0   3厘米

彩图一九四　八区下层出土A型漆奁（M1Ⅷ：4212）奁盖

0 ┣━━━┿━━━┫ 3厘米

彩图一九五　八区下层出土A型漆奁（M1Ⅷ：4212）

0　　　　　　3厘米

彩图一九六　九区下层出土A型漆耳杯（M1Ⅸ：4857）

0   3厘米

彩图一九七　九区下层出土C型漆耳杯（M1Ⅸ：4959）

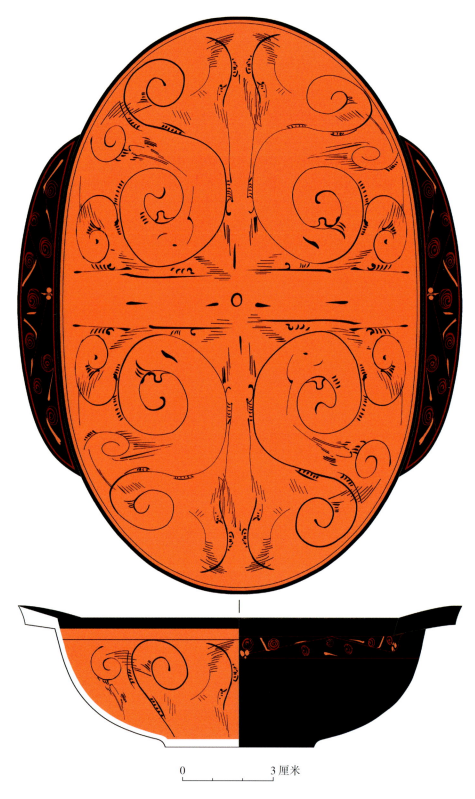

0   3 厘米

彩图一九八　九区下层出土 D 型漆耳杯（M1IX：4991）

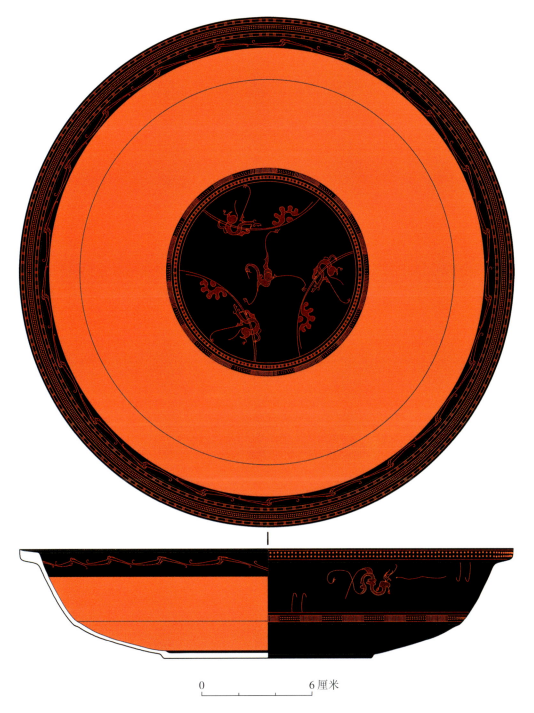

0   6厘米

彩图一九九　九区下层出土A型漆盘（M1Ⅸ：3569）

0 _____ 3 厘米

彩图二〇〇　九区下层出土H型漆盘（M1Ⅸ∶4742）

彩图二〇一　九区下层出土I型漆盘（M1IX：5849）

0 ____ 3厘米

0   3厘米

彩图二○二 十区下层出土A型漆耳杯（M1 X：4598）

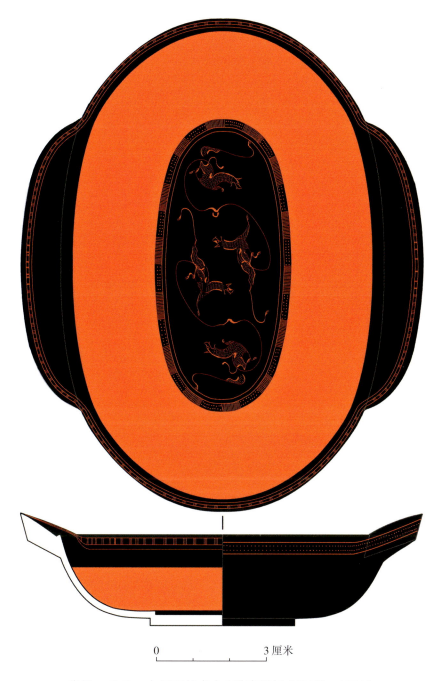

0   3厘米

彩图二〇三　十区下层出土A型漆耳杯（M1X：3574）

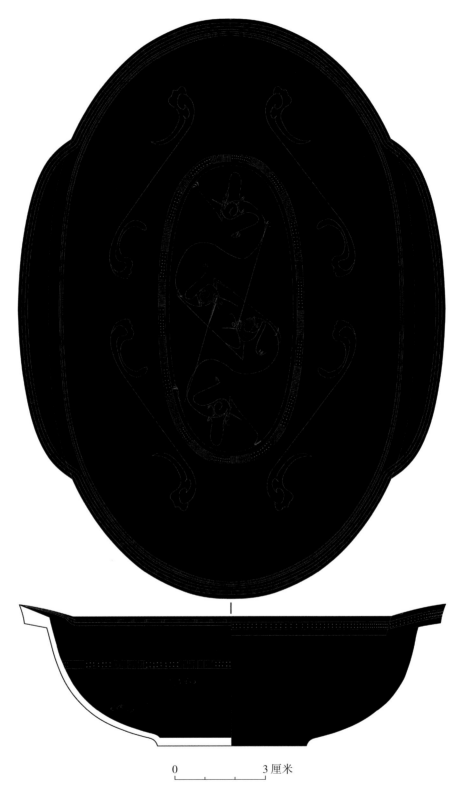

0 _____ 3厘米

彩图二○四 十区下层出土C型漆耳杯（M1X：4572）

0   3厘米

彩图二〇五　十区下层出土C型漆耳杯（M1X：4940）

0   6厘米

彩图二〇六 十区下层出土A型漆盘（M1 X：4771）

0　　　　　　　3厘米

彩图二〇七　十区下层出土A型漆盘（M1Ⅹ：3577）

0   3 厘米

彩图二〇八　十区下层出土H型漆盘（M1 X：4780）

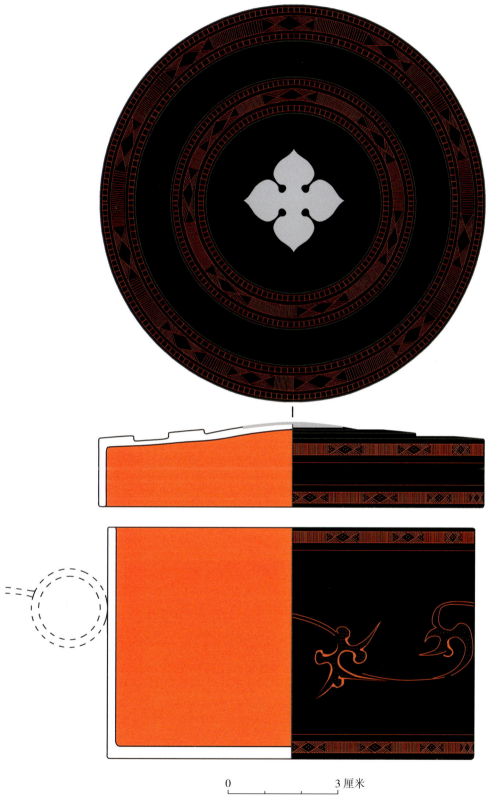

0　　　　　　　3厘米

彩图二〇九　十区下层出土A型漆卮（M1Ⅹ：4855）

0   3厘米

彩图二一〇 十区下层出土A型漆卮（M1Ⅹ：3578）

0　　　　　　3厘米

彩图二一一　十区下层出土A型漆厄（M1Ⅹ：4875）

0 ├─────────┤ 12 厘米

彩图二一二　十一区下层出土漆笥（M1Ⅺ：2620）

彩　版

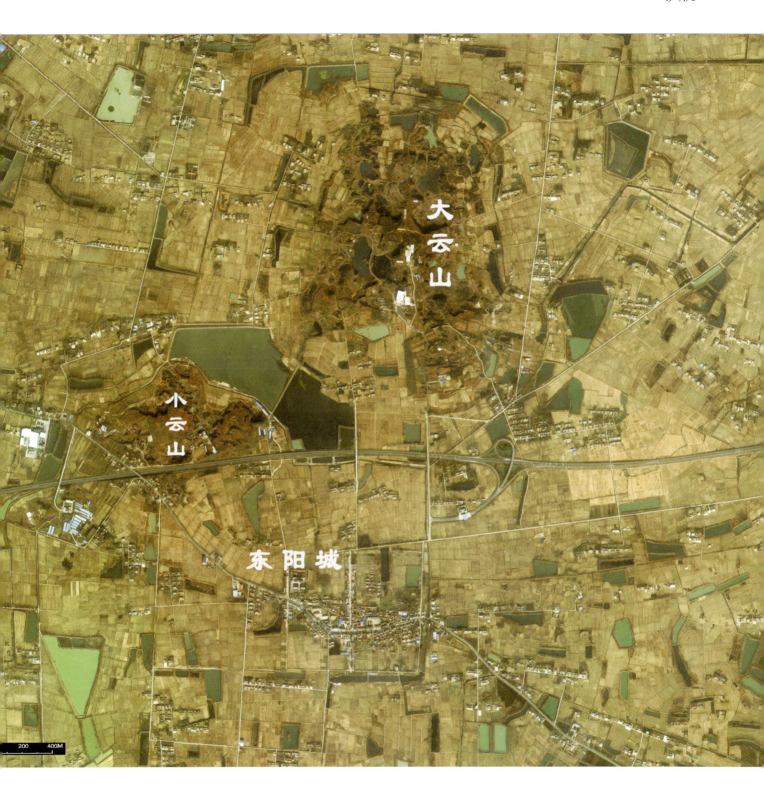

大云山江都王陵位置卫星图

1. 大云山远眺（由东向西）

2. 发掘前环境

大云山远眺及发掘前环境

暗葬坑

暗葬坑

M8

M2

M1

车马坑

大云山汉墓陵园

大云山1号汉墓发掘现场及工作照

2 号墓

1 号墓

1号墓与2号墓（航拍）

1. 发掘前龙塘近景

2. 1号墓、2号墓封土剖面及叠压关系（由南向北）

发掘前龙塘近景，1号墓、2号墓封土剖面及叠压关系

1号墓墓圹（由北向南）

1号墓南墓道（由北向南）

1号墓南墓道开口（由南向北）

1. 南墓道底部加工遗迹（由北向南）

2. 南墓道东壁上部土坯砌筑遗迹（由西向东）

1号墓南墓道遗迹

1号墓南墓道东壁（由北向南）

1. 南墓道东侧土坯修补平面遗迹

2. 南墓道东侧土坯堆放遗迹

1号墓南墓道遗迹

1. 南墓道石础及基槽侧面（由东向西）

2. 南墓道东壁用石片修补遗迹

1号墓南墓道遗迹

1.南墓道东侧壁龛

2.北墓道西壁土坯修整遗迹

1号墓南墓道及北墓道

1号墓北墓道（由南向北）

1号墓墓室（左北右南）

1号墓墓室开口及基槽位置（左北右南）

1号墓墓室东、西壁清理后（由南向北）

1. 墓室西壁下部壁面修补遗迹

2. 南墓道填土解剖

1号墓墓室西壁遗迹，南墓道填土

1. 南墓道填土中出土夯锤

2. 北墓道填土层面夯窝遗迹

3. 北墓道现代盗洞

1号墓南墓道和北墓道填土，北墓道现代盗洞

1. 墓室古代盗坑

2. 墓室近北墓道口填土剖面（由南向北）

1号墓墓室古代盗坑，墓室近北墓道口填土

1.墓室近南墓道口填土剖面

2.墓室西南角盗坑塌方剖面遗迹

1号墓墓室近南墓道口填土，墓室西南角盗坑

1号墓墓室内积炭（由北向南）

1. 墓室东北角铁凿出土情况

2. 墓底积炭（由南向北）

1号墓墓室东北角铁凿出土情况及墓底积炭

1号墓墓室清理前椁室（由南向北）

1号墓盗坑底部棺椁木板

1. 木锛出土情况

2. 圆木出土情况

1号墓盗坑内遗物出土情况

1. 用圆木与木桩制作的围挡

2. 竹簸箕出土情况

1号墓盗坑内围挡及竹簸箕出土情况

1. 竹绳出土情况

2. 木甬出土情况

1号墓盗坑内遗物出土情况

1. 椁室清理后（由南向北）

2. 南墓道枋木

1号墓椁室及南墓道枋木

1号墓黄肠题凑及底板（由北向南）

1. 黄肠题凑与外侧立柱

2. 黄肠题凑与内侧立柱

1号墓黄肠题凑与立柱

1. 黄肠题凑南大门

2. 黄肠题凑南大门暗栓卯眼

3. 黄肠题凑东南转角细部

1号墓黄肠题凑

1. 外椁现存西侧板

2. 外椁西侧板榫卯

1号墓外椁

1. 外椁门（由北向南）

2. 中椁立柱

1号墓外椁门、中椁立柱

1. 内椁门

2. 内椁

1号墓内椁门、内椁

1号墓内棺（玉棺）出土情况

1. 外棺残片

2. 亚腰形铜构件出土情况

1号墓外棺及遗物出土情况

1. 外回廊（清理后　由南向北）

2. 外回廊底板上立柱

1号墓外回廊

1. 外回廊立柱与侧板结构

2. 外回廊底部芦席遗迹

1号墓外回廊

1. K11（清理后　由南向北）

2. K11填土解剖后夯窝遗迹

1号墓K11

1. 瓷豆（M1BT：1）

2. 瓷豆（M1BT：2）

3. 瓦当（M1FT：1）

4. 瓦当（M1FT：2）

瓷豆，瓦当

1. 铁臿（M1FT：3）

2. 铁斧（M1FT：4）

3. 瓷钵（M1DK③：31）

4. 瓷豆（M1DK③：30）

5. 瓷豆（M1DK③：33）

6. 瓷罐（M1DK③：1）

铁臿、斧，瓷钵、豆、罐

1. 瓷罐（M1DK③：32）

2. 瓷碗（M1DK③：3）

3. 瓷碗（M1DK③：4）

4. 瓷碗（M1DK③：5）

5. 瓷碗（M1DK③：7）

6. 瓷碗（M1DK③：16）

瓷罐、碗

1. 瓷碗（M1DK③：19）

2. 瓷碗（M1DK③：26）

3. 瓷碗（M1DK③：21）

4. 瓷碗（M1DK③：27）

5. 瓷碗（M1DK③：34）

6. 瓷盅（M1DK③：6）

瓷碗、盅

1. 瓷盏（M1DK③：15）

3. 石造像（M1DK③：8）

2. 瓷盏（M1DK③：25）

4. 石砚（M1DK③：22）

瓷盏，石造像、砚

1. 构件（M1DK③：9）

2. 构件（M1DK③：18）

3. 造像（M1DK③：12）正视

4. 造像（M1DK③：12）侧视

陶构件、造像

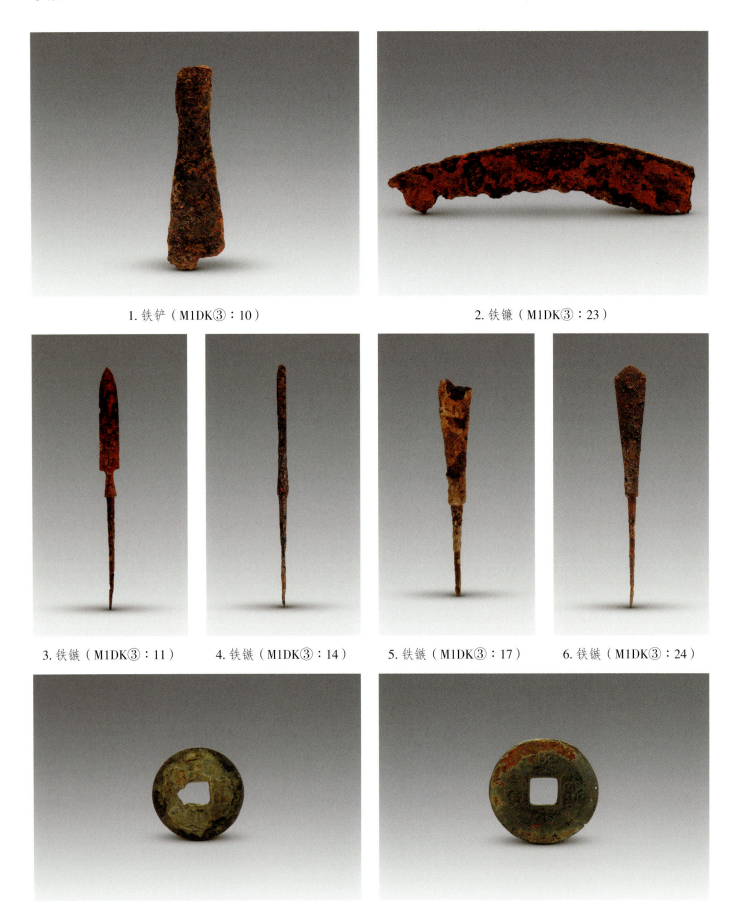

1. 铁铲（M1DK③：10）　　　　　　　　　　2. 铁镰（M1DK③：23）

3. 铁镞（M1DK③：11）　　4. 铁镞（M1DK③：14）　　5. 铁镞（M1DK③：17）　　6. 铁镞（M1DK③：24）

7. 铜钱（M1DK③：20）　　　　　　　　　　8. 铜钱（M1DK③：29）

铁铲、镰、镞，铜钱

1号墓盗坑下层出土遗物（由北向南）

1. 铜戈出土情况

2. 铜犀牛、大象、鼎、锺、钫、罐、匜、勺、杵、白及银盒、玉圭、石砚出土情况

1号墓盗坑下层出土遗物

1. 铜铺首出土情况

2. 盗洞东部金饰件出土情况

1号墓盗坑下层出土遗物

1号墓盗坑下层出土玉贝带

1号墓盗坑下层出土玉贝带

1. 盗洞东南角漆奁、漆卮、玉鱼出土情况

2. 盗洞东北角木车轮出土情况

1号墓盗坑下层出土遗物

1. E型盖弓帽（M1DK⑥：389）

2. E型盖弓帽（M1DK⑥：397）

3. B型带扣（M1DK⑥：345）

4. C型带扣（M1DK⑥：27）

5. A型泡饰（M1DK⑥：175）

6. A型泡饰（M1DK⑥：360）

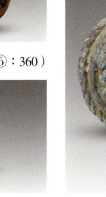

9. C型泡饰（M1DK⑥：731）

7. A型泡饰（M1DK⑥：450）

8. C型泡饰（M1DK⑥：566）

10. A型节约（M1DK⑥：348）

铜盖弓帽、带扣、泡饰

A型铜戈（M1DK⑥：579）

1. A型（M1DK⑥：582）

2. B型（M1DK⑥：622）

铜戈

A型铜矛（M1DK⑥：623）

A型铜矛（M1DK⑥：624）

A型铜矛（M1DK⑥：625）

A型铜矛（M1DK⑥：626）

A型铜矛（M1DK⑥：627）

1. A型（M1DK⑥：69）　　　　　　　　　　2. A型（M1DK⑥：157）

3. C型（M1DK⑥：922）　　　　4. C型（M1DK⑥：438）　　　　5. D型（M1DK⑥：1741）

铜镦

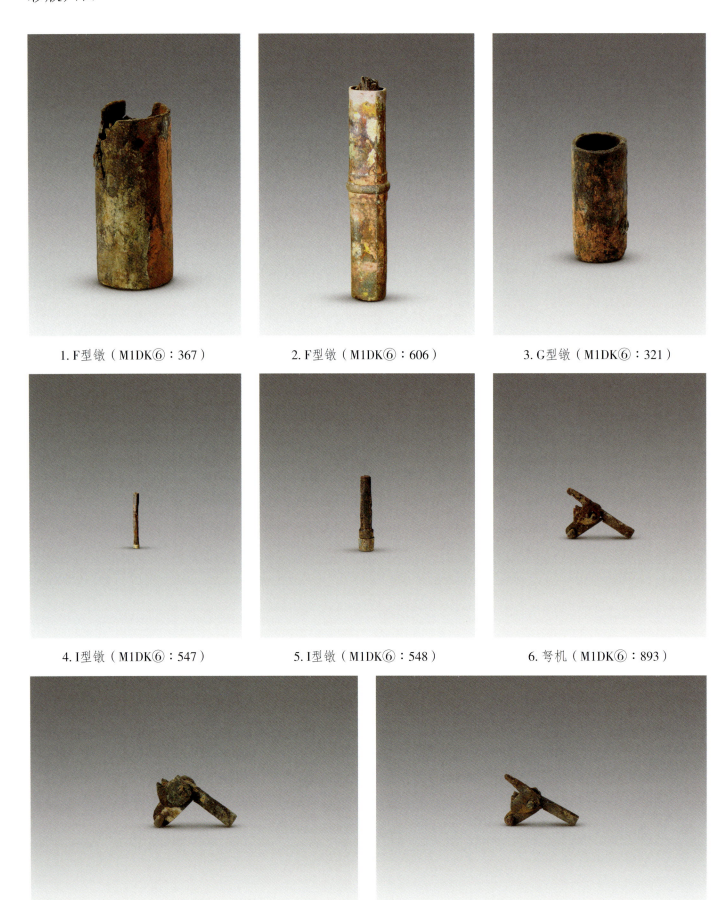

铜镦、弩机

1. F型镦（M1DK⑥：367）　　　2. F型镦（M1DK⑥：606）　　　3. G型镦（M1DK⑥：321）

4. I型镦（M1DK⑥：547）　　　5. I型镦（M1DK⑥：548）　　　6. 弩机（M1DK⑥：893）

7. B型弩机（M1DK⑥：967）　　　　　　　8. B型弩机（M1DK⑥：1646）

铜镦、弩机

1. D型（M1DK⑥：34）

2. I型（M1DK⑥：2144）

3. I型（M1DK⑥：2149）

4. I型（M1DK⑥：1835、M1DK⑥：969、M1DK⑥：1195、M1DK⑥：927、M1DK⑥：2148）

5. O型（M1DK⑥：1901）

6. P型（M1DK⑥：888）

7. Q型（M1DK⑥：798）

铜镞

1. Q型镞（M1DK⑥：229、M1DK⑥：811、M1DK⑥：804、M1DK⑥：823） 　　2. R型镞（M1DK⑥：227）

3. 钺（M1DK⑥：928）

铜镞、钺

铜纽钟（M1DK⑥：576）

铜纽钟（M1DK⑥：576）

1. M1DK⑥：629

2. M1DK⑥：919

铜錞于

铜錞于（M1DK⑥：395）

1. 顶部纹饰

2. 肩部纹饰

3. 口部纹饰

铜錞于（M1DK⑥：395）

铜錞于（M1DK⑥：395）右边铭文

铜錞于（M1DK⑥：395）左边铭文

1. M1DK⑥出土铜器

2. 鼎盖（M1DK⑥：1393）

铜器

1. M1DK⑥：665

2. M1DK⑥：666、M1DK⑥：667、M1DK⑥：668、M1DK⑥：1287

A型铜鼎

1. A型锺（M1DK⑥：662）

3. A型钫（M1DK⑥：656）

2. A型锺（M1DK⑥：663、M1DK⑥：664、M1DK⑥：1288、M1DK⑥：1289）

A型铜锺、钫

1. A型钫（M1DK⑥：657、M1DK⑥：658、M1DK⑥：659、M1DK⑥：660）

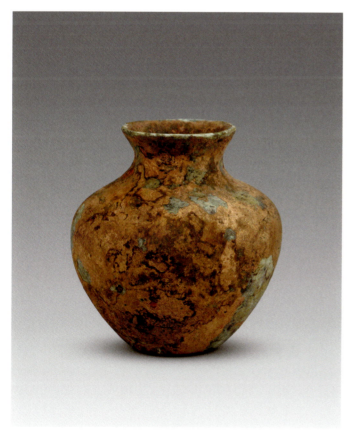

2. 罐（M1DK⑥：669）

3. 匜（M1DK⑥：677）

铜钫、罐、匜

1. 匜（M1DK⑥：688、M1DK⑥：689、M1DK⑥：695、M1DK⑥：696）

2. A型勺（M1DK⑥：690）

3. A型勺（M1DK⑥：691～M1DK⑥：694）

铜匜、勺

1. 杵（M1DK⑥：672）

3. 臼杯（M1DK⑥：618）

2. 杵（M1DK⑥：673~M1DK⑥：676）

4. 臼杯（M1DK⑥：619、M1DK⑥：647~M1DK⑥：649）

铜杵、臼杯

铜镜（M1DK⑥：1402-8）

铜镜（M1DK⑥：1404-8）

铜镜（M1DK⑥：1406）

铜镜（M1DK⑥：1414-1）

1. A型（M1DK⑥：2174）

2. A型（M1DK⑥：2175~M1DK⑥：2193）

3. B型（M1DK⑥：2223）

4. B型（M1DK⑥：2223）细部

铜刷

1. B型刷（M1DK⑥：2224~M1K1⑥：2244）

2. C型刷（M1DK⑥：1398）

3. C型刷（M1DK⑥：1398、M1DK⑥：2278~M1DK⑥：2288）

铜刷

1. A型刷柄（M1DK⑥：1399）

2. A型刷柄（M1DK⑥：2272）

3. A型刷柄（M1DK⑥：2273）

4. B型刷柄（M1DK⑥：2274）

5. B型刷柄（M1DK⑥：2275）

6. B型刷柄（M1DK⑥：2276）

7. 尺（M1DK⑥：560）

铜刷柄、尺

1. A型带钩（M1DK⑥：333）

2. A型带钩（M1DK⑥：571）

3. A型带钩（M1DK⑥：575）

4. B型带钩（M1DK⑥：1293）

5. B型带钩（M1DK⑥：1294~M1DK⑥：1303）

铜带钩

1. A型（M1DK⑥：553）

2. D型（M1DK⑥：1291）

铜镇

铜犀牛（M1DK⑥：620）

铜犀牛（M1DK⑥：620）

铜驯犀俑（M1DK⑥：686）

铜象、驯象俑（M1DK⑥：621、M1DK⑥：687）

铜象（M1DK⑥：621）

1. 象（M1DK⑥：621）

2. 驯象俑（M1DK⑥：687）

铜象、驯象俑

A型铜铺首（M1DK⑥：1601）

1. M1DK⑥：208

2. M1DK⑥：607

3. M1DK⑥：933

4. M1DK⑥：1600

A型铜铺首

1. A型（M1DK⑥：1602）

2. B型（M1DK⑥：21）

3. B型（M1DK⑥：138）

4. B型（M1DK⑥：169）

铜铺首

1. M1DK⑥：353

2. M1DK⑥：353侧视

3. M1DK⑥：483

4. M1DK⑥：590

B型铜铺首

1. B型（M1DK⑥：929）

2. B型（M1DK⑥：934）

3. G型（M1DK⑥：170）

4. H型（M1DK⑥：589）

铜铺首

1. I型铺首（M1DK⑥：506）

2. J型铺首（M1DK⑥：375）

3. A型环（M1DK⑥：598）

4. A型环（M1DK⑥：464）

5. A型环（M1DK⑥：376）

6. B型环（M1DK⑥：325）

铜铺首、环

1. 构件（M1DK⑥：1405）

2. 构件（M1DK⑥：604）

3. 构件（M1DK⑥：1286）

5. 亚腰形构件（M1DK⑥：140）

4. 构件（M1DK⑥：1290）

6. 亚腰形构件（M1DK⑥：433）

铜构件

1. 锥形器（M1DK⑥：471）

2. 锥形器（M1DK⑥：851）

3. 锥形器（M1DK⑥：475-1）

4. 龙首形饰（M1DK⑥：778）

5. 龙首形饰（M1DK⑥：853）

6. 龙首形饰（M1DK⑥：861）

铜锥形器、龙首形饰

1. 饰件（M1DK⑥：96）

2. 饰件（M1DK⑥：480）

3. 饰件（M1DK⑥：2289）

4. 扣饰（M1DK⑥：388）

5. 扣饰（M1DK⑥：388）侧视

铜饰件、扣饰

1. 扣饰（M1DK⑥：467）

2. 扣饰（M1DK⑥：467-1）

3. 扣饰（M1DK⑥：457）

4. 卮持（M1DK⑥：474）

5. B型算珠形饰（M1DK⑥：135）

铜扣饰、卮持、算珠形饰

铜扣饰（M1DK⑥：2290）

2. B型矛（M1DK⑥：573）

1. A型矛（M1DK⑥：585）

3. B型铍（M1DK⑥：858）

4. 铍（M1DK⑥：478）

5. 铍（M1DK⑥：479）

铁矛、铍

1. A型（M1DK⑥：1418）

2. A型（M1DK⑥：1420）

3. B型（M1DK⑥：1417）

4. B型（M1DK⑥：1421）

铁刀

1. C型剑（M1DK⑥：330-1）

2. C型剑（M1DK⑥：330-4、M1DK⑥：330-39）

3. 凿（M1DK⑥：1481）　　4. 凿（M1DK⑥：1425）　　5. B型钉（M1DK⑥：383）　　6. B型钉（M1DK⑥：469）

铁剑、凿、钉

1. 斧（M1DK⑥：1413）

2. 锤（M1DK⑥：1422）

3. 锤（M1DK⑥：1423）

4. 锤（M1DK⑥：1412）

5. 甴（M1DK⑥：608）

6. 甴（M1DK⑥：93）

7. 甴（M1DK⑥：220）

铁斧、锤、甴

1. A型铁削（M1DK⑥：1292）

2. D型铁削（M1DK⑥：460）

3. 铁环首器（M1DK⑥：427）

4. 金饰件（M1DK⑥：327）

铁削、环首器，金饰件

1. A型（M1DK⑥：327-1）　　　2. A型（M1DK⑥：327-20）　　　3. A型（M1DK⑥：327-21）

4. A型（M1DK⑥：327-22）　　　　　　　5. B型（M1DK⑥：327-3）

6. B型（M1DK⑥：327-14）

金饰件

1. M1DK⑥：327-9

2. M1DK⑥：327-4

3. M1DK⑥：327-5

C型金饰件

1. M1DK⑥：327-8

2. M1DK⑥：327-10

3. M1DK⑥：327-7

C型金饰件

1. M1DK⑥：327-19

2. M1DK⑥：327-2

3. M1DK⑥：327-11

C型金饰件

1. M1DK⑥：327-12

2. M1DK⑥：327-13

3. M1DK⑥：327-6

C型金饰件

1. M1DK⑥：327-15

2. M1DK⑥：327-16

3. M1DK⑥：327-17

4. M1DK⑥：327-18

C型金饰件

1. 金箔饰（M1DK⑥：1-3-4、M1DK⑥：1-3-1、M1DK⑥：1-3-7、M1DK⑥：1-3-5、M1DK⑥：1-3-2）

2. 银合页（M1DK⑥：23）

3. 银合页（M1DK⑥：612）

4. 银泡饰（M1DK⑥：233）

5. 银箔饰（M1DK⑥：1-4-3、M1DK⑥：1-4-4、M1DK⑥：1-4-6、
M1DK⑥：1-4-1、M1DK⑥：1-4-5、M1DK⑥：1-4-2）

金箔饰，银合页、泡饰、箔饰

1. A型（M1DK⑥：161）

2. B型（M1DK⑥：584）

3. B型（M1DK⑥：580）正视

4. B型（M1DK⑥：580）侧视

银镦

银盒（M1DK⑥：661）

1. 玉棺片饰（M1DK⑥：1-1-2）

2. 玉棺片饰（M1DK⑥：1-1-9）

3. 玉棺片饰（M1DK⑥：1-1-11）

4. 玉棺片饰（M1DK⑥：1-1-26）

5. 玉棺璧饰（M1DK⑥：1-2-2）

玉棺片饰、璧饰

1. 玉棺璧饰（M1DK⑥：1-2-5）

2. 玉棺璧饰（M1DK⑥：1-2-6）

3. 玉棺璧饰（M1DK⑥：1-2-12）

4. 玉棺璧饰（M1DK⑥：1-2-13）

5. 玉棺璧饰（M1DK⑥：1-2-14）

6. 镶玉漆棺残片（M1DK⑥：829-1）

玉棺璧饰，镶玉漆棺残片

1. M1DK⑥：434-1

2. M1DK⑥：434-2

镶玉漆棺残片

1. M1DK⑥：2-1

2. M1DK⑥：2-3

3. M1DK⑥：2-5正面

4. M1DK⑥：2-5背面

5. M1DK⑥：2-16

6. M1DK⑥：2-18

玉衣片

1. M1DK⑥：2-34~M1DK⑥：37

2. M1DK⑥：2-56

3. M1DK⑥：2-72、M1DK⑥：73

4. M1DK⑥：2-88

5. M1DK⑥：2-106

6. M1DK⑥：2-107

7. M1DK⑥：2-108

8. M1DK⑥：113~M1DK⑥：115

玉衣片

1. M1DK⑥：2-116、M1DK⑥：2-117

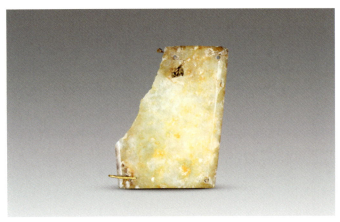

2. M1DK⑥：2-118

3. M1DK⑥：2-120

4. M1DK⑥：盗洞内

玉衣片

1. M1DK⑥：613

2. M1DK⑥：614

3. M1DK⑥：615

4. M1DK⑥：616

5. M1DK⑥：617

玉圭

1. M1DK⑥：78

2. M1DK⑥：156

3. M1DK⑥：514

4. M1DK⑥：535

玉璧

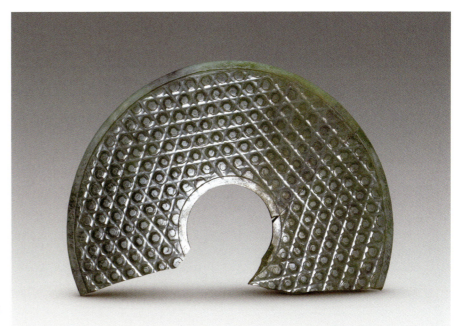

1. M1DK⑥：727

2. M1DK⑥：728

3. M1DK⑥：747

玉璧

1. 璧（M1DK⑥：763）

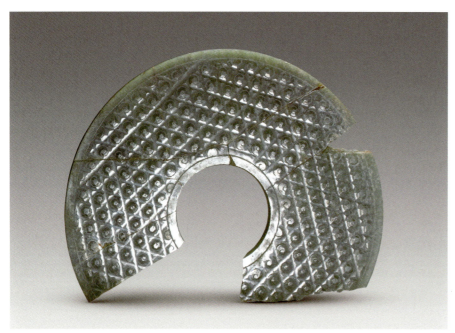

2. 璧（M1DK⑥：1778）

3. 璜（M1DK⑥：15）

玉璧、璜

1. M1DK⑥：153

2. M1DK⑥：435

3. M1DK⑥：526

玉璜

1. 璜（M1DK⑥：832）

2. 璜（M1DK⑥：1770）

3. 环（M1DK⑥：57）

4. 环（M1DK⑥：71）

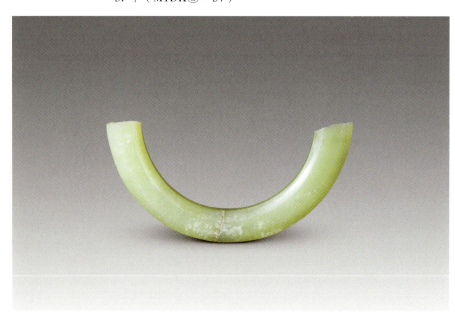

5. 环（M1DK⑥：94）

玉璜、环

1. 环（M1DK⑥：200）

2. 环（M1DK⑥：296）

3. 环（M1DK⑥：701）

4. 佩饰（M1DK⑥：116）

玉环、佩饰

1. M1DK⑥：63

2. M1DK⑥：91

玉佩饰

1. M1DK⑥：167

2. M1DK⑥：207

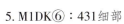

5. M1DK⑥：431细部

3. M1DK⑥：431

4. M1DK⑥：431

玉佩饰

1. M1DK⑥：362

2. M1DK⑥：706

3. M1DK⑥：752

4. M1DK⑥：755

5. M1DK⑥：862

玉佩饰

1. 佩饰（M1DK⑥：866）

2. 鱼（M1DK⑥：1408）

3. 塞（M1DK⑥：865、M1DK⑥：869、M1DK⑥：863、M1DK⑥：870）

玉佩饰、鱼、塞

1. 剑首（M1DK⑥：868）　　　　　　　2. 剑珌（M1DK⑥：796）

3. 戈（M1DK⑥：477）

玉剑首、剑珌、戈

1. 戈（M1DK⑥：628）

2. 耳杯（M1DK⑥：48）

3. 耳杯（M1DK⑥：118）

4. 碗（M1DK⑥：44）

5. 碗（M1DK⑥：733）

玉戈、耳杯、碗

1. 碗（M1DK⑥：50）

2. 卮（M1DK⑥：40）

3. 卮（M1DK⑥：41）　　　　　　　4. 卮（M1DK⑥：263）

玉碗、卮

1. 贝带（M1DK⑥：354）

2. 带板（M1DK⑥：354-1）

玉贝带、带板

1. 玉带板（M1DK⑥：354-2）

2. 玉带板（M1DK⑥：355-1）

3. 玛瑙贝形饰（M1DK⑥：354-3）　　4. 玉扣舌（M1DK⑥：355-3）　　5. 玉贝形饰（M1DK⑥：355-4）

玉带板、扣舌、贝形饰，玛瑙贝形饰

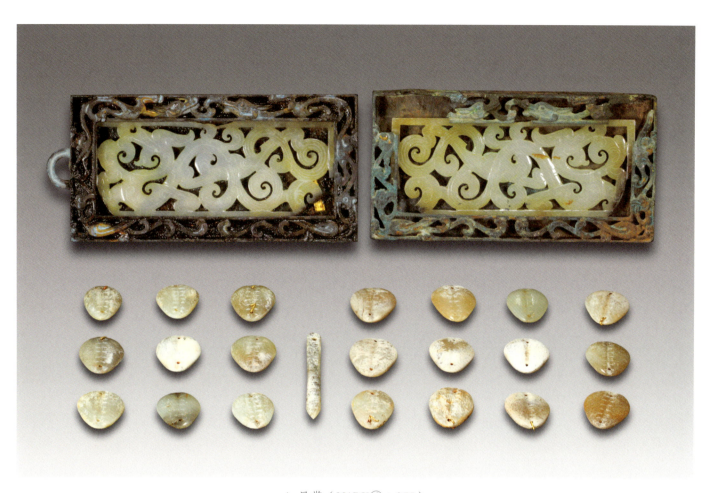

1. 贝带（M1DK⑥：355）

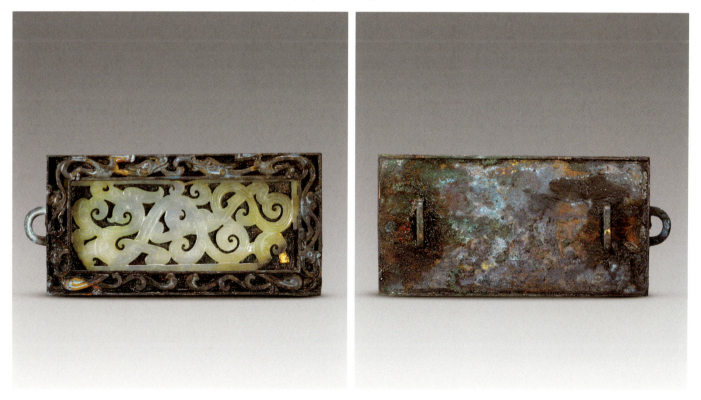

2. 带板（M1DK⑥：355-2）

玉贝带、带板

1. 玉牌饰（M1DK⑥：1586）

2. 玉器（M1DK⑥：43）

3. 玉器（M1DK⑥：871）

4. 石研（M1DK⑥：678）

5. 石研（M1DK⑥：1395）

6. 石器（M1DK⑥：445）

7. 玛瑙杯（M1DK⑥：285）

8. 玛瑙串饰（M1DK⑥：864）

玉牌饰，玉器，石研，石器，玛瑙杯、串饰

1. 圆形子奁盖（M1DK⑥：1404-2）

3. 马蹄形子奁（M1DK⑥：1404-7）

2. 椭圆形子奁（M1DK⑥：1404-3）

漆奁

漆卮（M1DK⑥：356）

1. M1DK⑥：3

2. M1DK⑥：4

3. M1DK⑥：5

4. M1DK⑥：6

5. M1DK⑥：9

6. M1DK⑥：10

木耜

1. M1DK⑥：11

2. M1DK⑥：12

3. M1DK⑥：13

4. M1DK⑥：14

5. M1DK⑥：213

6. M1DK⑥：214

木耜

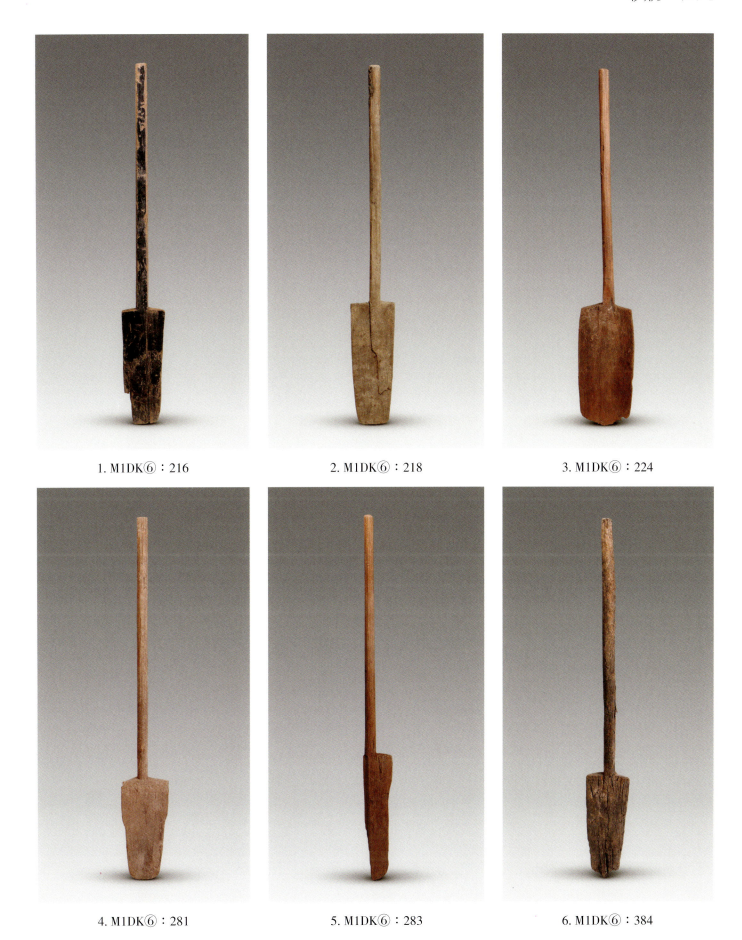

1. M1DK⑥：216

2. M1DK⑥：218

3. M1DK⑥：224

4. M1DK⑥：281

5. M1DK⑥：283

6. M1DK⑥：384

木臿

1. 木车轮（M1DK⑥：248）

3. 木锛（M1DK⑥：222）

4. 灰陶钵（M1DK⑥：7）

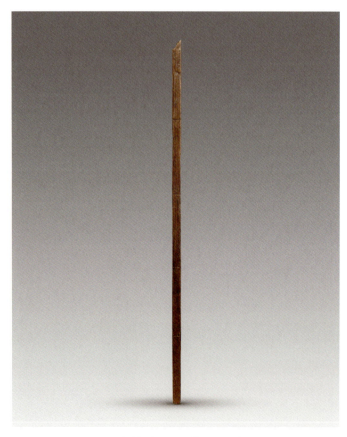

2. 木尺（M1DK⑥：212）

5. 灰陶钵（M1DK⑥：17）

木车轮、尺、锛，灰陶钵

1. B型罐（M1DK⑥：328）

2. B型壶（M1DK⑥：454）

釉陶罐、壶

大云山

西汉江都王陵 1 号墓发掘报告

（四）

南　京　博　物　院
盱眙县文化广电和旅游局　编著

主　编　李则斌
副主编　陈　刚　左　骏

文物出版社

北京·2020

EXCAVATION REPORT ON THE KING OF JIANGDU'S TOMB M1 OF THE WESTERN HAN PERIOD AT DAYUNSHAN

(IV)

by

Nanjing Museum

and

Xuyi County Bureau of Culture, Broadcast, Television and Tourism

EDITOR – IN – CHIEF: LI Zebin

DEPUTY EDITOR – IN – CHIEFS: CHEN Gang　ZUO Jun

Cultural Relics Press

Beijing · 2020

彩　版（续）

1. 甾（M1：5092）　　　　2. 夯锤（M1：5093）　　　　3. 夯锤（M1：5187）

4. 凿（M1：5089）　　　　5. 凿（M1：5099）　　　　6. 凿（M1：5101）

铁甾、夯锤、凿

铁凿

1. M1：5119

2. M1：5080

3. M1：5094

4. M1：5096

5. M1：5100

6. M1：5118

1. 东回廊上层出土遗物（由北向南）　　　　　　　　2. 西回廊上层出土遗物（由北向南）

东回廊上层和西回廊上层出土遗物

1. A型车軎（M1Ⅰ：1557）

2. C型车軎（M1Ⅰ：2175-1）

3. C型车軎（M1Ⅰ：2175-1）

4. C型车軎（M1Ⅰ：1667）

5. 釭（M1Ⅰ：2175-2）

6. 铜（M1Ⅰ：2175-3）

铜车軎、釭、铜

1. A 型辕首（M1Ⅰ：280）

2. B 型辕首（M1Ⅰ：1555）

3. B 型辕首（M1Ⅰ：3687）

铜辕首

1. A型轊（M1Ⅰ：1556）

2. B型轊（M1Ⅰ：75）

3. A型帽饰（M1Ⅰ：2153、M1Ⅰ：2173）

4. A型帽饰（M1Ⅰ：2153、M1Ⅰ：2173）正视

5. 兽首构件（M1Ⅰ：1506）

6. 伏兔（M1Ⅰ：2158）

7. A型钩（M1Ⅰ：1679）

铜轊、帽饰、兽首构件、伏兔、钩

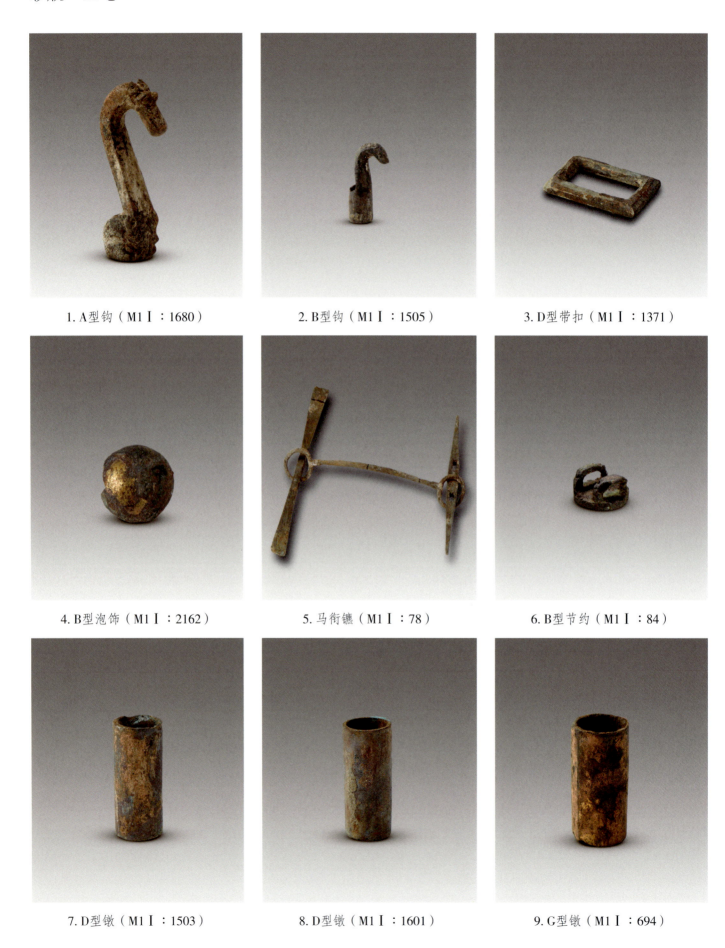

1. A型钩（M1Ⅰ：1680）　　　2. B型钩（M1Ⅰ：1505）　　　3. D型带扣（M1Ⅰ：1371）

4. B型泡饰（M1Ⅰ：2162）　　　5. 马衔镳（M1Ⅰ：78）　　　6. B型节约（M1Ⅰ：84）

7. D型镦（M1Ⅰ：1503）　　　8. D型镦（M1Ⅰ：1601）　　　9. G型镦（M1Ⅰ：694）

铜钩、带扣、泡饰、马衔镳、节约、镦

1. M1 I：1365

2. M1 I：3742

A型铜弩机

1. M1 I ：1668

2. M1 I ：2165

A型铜承弓器

1. 铜衔环（M1Ⅰ：693）

2. A型铜环（M1Ⅰ：1666）

3. 银饰件（M1Ⅰ：1368）

4. 银饰件（M1Ⅰ：1369）

铜衔环、环，银饰件

1. 出土遗物

2. 铁镞、弩机

二区上层出土遗物

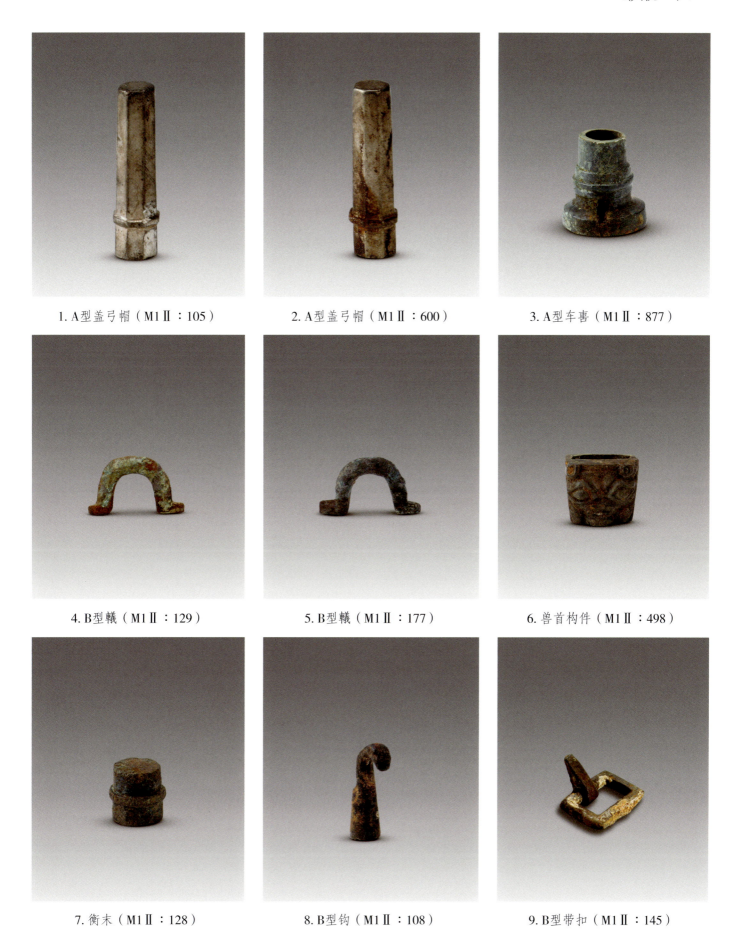

1. A型盖弓帽（M1Ⅱ：105）　　　2. A型盖弓帽（M1Ⅱ：600）　　　3. A型车䡓（M1Ⅱ：877）

4. B型轙（M1Ⅱ：129）　　　5. B型轙（M1Ⅱ：177）　　　6. 兽首构件（M1Ⅱ：498）

7. 衡末（M1Ⅱ：128）　　　8. B型钩（M1Ⅱ：108）　　　9. B型带扣（M1Ⅱ：145）

铜盖弓帽、车䡓、轙、兽首构件、衡末、钩、带扣

1. D型带扣（M1Ⅱ：3924）

2. 马衔镳（M1Ⅱ：601）

3. D型镦（M1Ⅱ：1564）

4. D型镦（M1Ⅱ：111）

5. D型镦（M1Ⅱ：1565）

6. D型镦（M1Ⅱ：1596）

铜带扣、马衔镳、镦

1. A型（M1Ⅱ：700）

2. B型（M1Ⅱ：92）

3. B型（M1Ⅱ：701）

4. B型（M1Ⅱ：703）

5. B型（M1Ⅱ：710）

铜弩机

1. B型弩机（M1Ⅱ：711）

2. B型弩机（M1Ⅱ：714）

3. B型弩机（M1Ⅱ：717）

4. B型弩机（M1Ⅱ：723）

5. B型弩机（M1Ⅱ：749）

6. S型镞（M1Ⅱ：5543、M1Ⅱ：5542）

铜弩机、镞

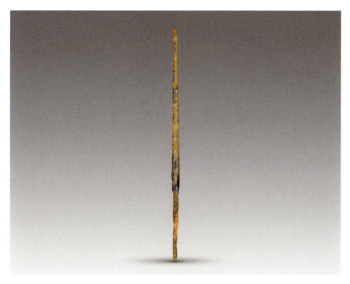

1. C型铁镞（M1Ⅱ：725）

2. C型铁镞（M1Ⅱ：5697~M1Ⅱ：5745）

3. C型铁镞（M1Ⅱ：5746~M1Ⅱ：5774）

4. C型铁镞（M1Ⅱ：5897~M1Ⅱ：6025）

5. 泥弹丸（M1Ⅱ：156）

铁镞，泥弹丸

三A区上层出土遗物

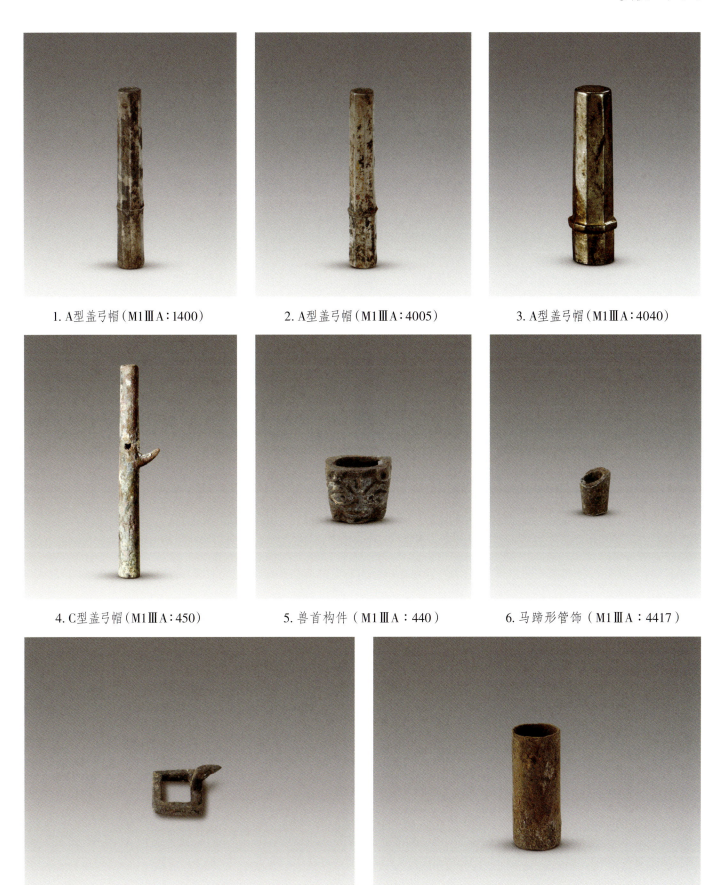

1. A型盖弓帽（M1ⅢA：1400）　　2. A型盖弓帽（M1ⅢA：4005）　　3. A型盖弓帽（M1ⅢA：4040）

4. C型盖弓帽（M1ⅢA：450）　　5. 兽首构件（M1ⅢA：440）　　6. 马蹄形管饰（M1ⅢA：4417）

7. B型带扣（M1ⅢA：4091）　　8. D型镦（M1ⅢA：4010）

铜盖弓帽、兽首构件、马蹄形管饰、带扣、镦

1. A型弩机（M1ⅢA：1403）

2. O型镞（M1ⅢA：4039）

3. 衔环（M1ⅢA：1421）

4. 铁釭（M1：3703）

铜弩机、镞、衔环，铁釭

三B区上层出土遗物

1. C型铜盖弓帽（M1ⅢB：210）　　2. C型铜盖弓帽（M1ⅢB：214）　　3. 铜伞柄箍饰（M1ⅢB：222）

4. 铜马蹄形管饰（M1ⅢB：234）　5. 铜马蹄形管饰（M1ⅢB：1412）　6. B型铜钩（M1ⅢB：429）　7. B型铜节约（M1ⅢB：228）

8. A型铜环（M1ⅢB：223）　　9. A型铜环（M1ⅢB：426）　　10. 泥弹丸（M1ⅢB：209）

铜盖弓帽、伞柄箍饰、马蹄形管饰、钩、节约、环，泥弹丸

四A区上层出土遗物

1. 衡末（M1ⅣA：804）

3. A型节约（M1ⅣA：796）

2. 马衔镳（M1ⅣA：803）

4. A型弩机（M1ⅣA：818）

铜衡末、马衔镳、节约、弩机

1. A型铜带钩（M1ⅣA：824）

4. A型铜盖弓帽（M1ⅣB：424）

2. A型铜带钩（M1ⅣA：1019）

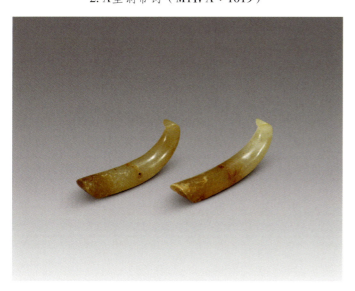

3. 玉钩饰（M1ⅣA：698、M1ⅣA：699）

5. 铜伞柄箍饰（M1ⅣB：578、M1ⅣB：279）

铜带钩、盖弓帽、伞柄箍饰，玉钩饰

1. 衡末（M1ⅣB：305）　　2. 衡末（M1ⅣB：919）　　3. A型带扣（M1ⅣB：862）

4. B型带扣（M1ⅣB：303）　　5. B型节约（M1ⅣB：244）　　6. B型节约（M1ⅣB：281）

7. B型节约（M1ⅣB：284）　　8. B型节约（M1ⅣB：916）　　9. B型节约（M1ⅣB：928）

铜衡末、带扣、节约

1. A型铜弩机（M1ⅣB：261）

2. B型铁戟（M1ⅣB：300）

3. B型铁戟（M1ⅣB：570、M1ⅣB：863、M1ⅣB：864、M1ⅣB：866）

4. C型铁镞（M1ⅣB：5648～M1ⅣB：5696）

铜弩机，铁戟、镞

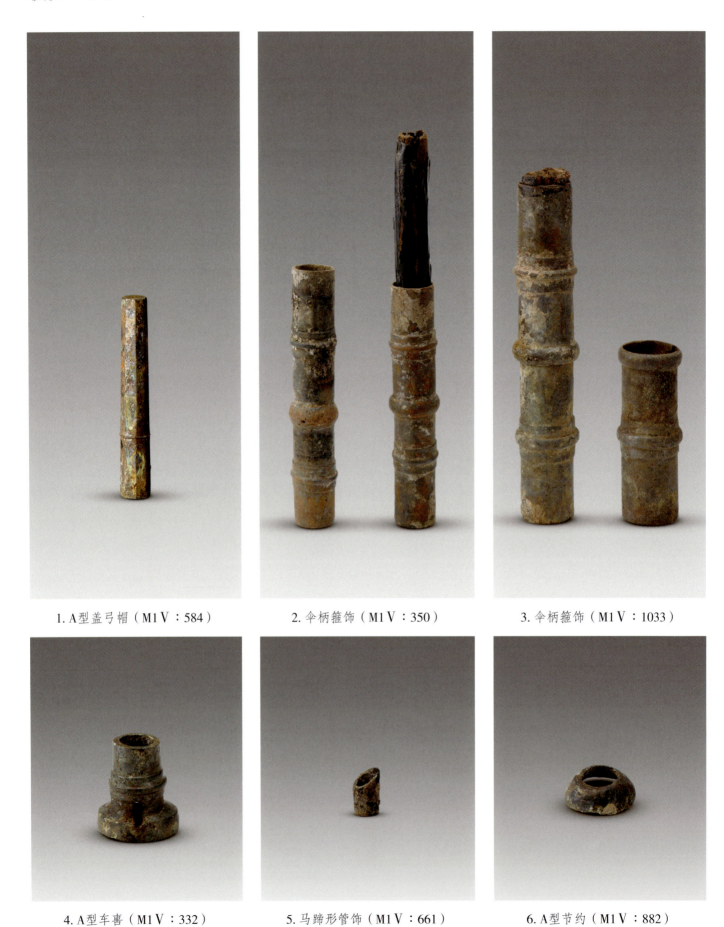

1. A型盖弓帽（M1 V：584）　　2. 伞柄箍饰（M1 V：350）　　3. 伞柄箍饰（M1 V：1033）

4. A型车軎（M1 V：332）　　5. 马蹄形管饰（M1 V：661）　　6. A型节约（M1 V：882）

铜盖弓帽、伞柄箍饰、车軎、马蹄形管饰、节约

1. A型铜带钩（M1Ⅴ：587）

2. 铁轙（M1Ⅴ：372）

3. 铁钩形器（M1Ⅴ：905）

4. 铁三叉形器（M1Ⅴ：336）

铜带钩，铁轙、钩形器、三叉形器

1. 出土遗物

2. 铜镦出土情况

六区上层出土遗物

1. 铜戟出土情况

2. 铜镞出土情况

六区上层出土遗物

1. 玉带钩、铁削出土情况

2. 水晶带钩出土情况

六区上层出土遗物

1. B型（M1Ⅵ：3765）　　2. D型（M1Ⅵ：988）　　3. D型（M1Ⅵ：987）

4. D型（M1Ⅵ：1000）　　5. D型（M1Ⅵ：1005）　　6. D型（M1Ⅵ：1323）

7. D型（M1Ⅵ：1807）　　8. D型（M1Ⅵ：5135）　　9. E型（M1Ⅵ：50）

铜盖弓帽

1. 伞柄箍饰（M1Ⅵ：3614、M1Ⅵ：3722）

2. 伞柄箍饰（M1Ⅵ：5219、M1Ⅵ：3612、M1Ⅵ：5143、M1Ⅵ：1001）

3. C型车軎（M1Ⅵ：978、M1Ⅵ：5116）

4. C型车軎（M1Ⅵ：979）

铜伞柄箍饰、车軎

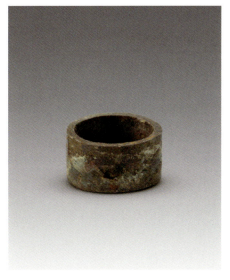

1. 铜（M1Ⅵ：1857）　　　　2. 铜（M1Ⅵ：3729）　　　　3. 铜（M1Ⅵ：3738）

4. A型辕首（M1Ⅵ：5146）

5. A型辕首（M1Ⅵ：5198）

铜锏、辕首

1. B型辕首（M1Ⅵ：1979）

2. B型辕首（M1Ⅵ：5117）

3. A型軨（M1Ⅵ：5140）　　　　　　　　4. A型軨（M1Ⅵ：5150）

铜辕首、軨

1. B型帽饰（M1Ⅵ：3626）

2. B型帽饰（M1Ⅵ：3788）

3. C型帽饰（M1Ⅵ：5229）

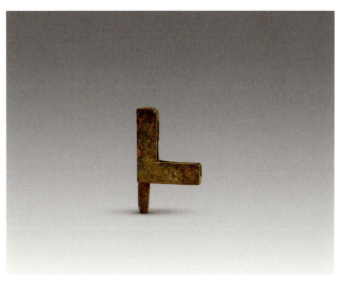

4. 门轴饰（M1Ⅵ：3775）

5. 马蹄形管饰（M1Ⅵ：3730）

6. 马蹄形管饰（M1Ⅵ：1978）

铜帽饰、门轴饰、马蹄形管饰

1. 伏兔（M1Ⅵ：1825）

2. 伏兔（M1Ⅵ：5132）

3. 轭足饰（M1Ⅵ：1806）

4. A型钩（M1Ⅵ：2011）

5. A型钩（M1Ⅵ：5181）

6. A型钩（M1Ⅵ：5194）

铜伏兔、轭足饰、钩

1. C型钩（M1Ⅵ：5196）

2. C型钩（M1Ⅵ：5142）

3. C型钩（M1Ⅵ：5231）

4. A型带扣（M1Ⅵ：972）

5. A型带扣（M1VI：5214）

6. A型带扣（M1VI：5215）

铜钩、带扣

1. B型带扣（M1Ⅵ：1762）　　　2. C型带扣（M1Ⅵ：1761）　　　3. B型泡饰（M1Ⅵ：1006）

4. B型当卢（M1Ⅵ：1867）

5. C型节约（M1Ⅵ：1003）　　6. C型节约（M1Ⅵ：2140）　　7. C型节约（M1Ⅵ：3624）　　8. C型节约（M1Ⅵ：3634）

铜带扣、泡饰、当卢、节约

1. A型（M1Ⅵ：5087）正面　　　　　2. A型（M1Ⅵ：5087）背面　　　　　3. B型（M1Ⅵ：5082）

铜矛

C型铜矛（M1Ⅵ：5085）

1. M1Ⅵ：5121

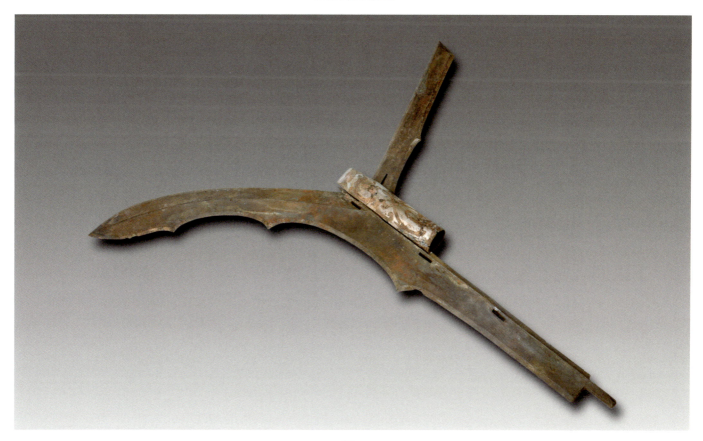

2. M1Ⅵ：5148

铜戟

A型铜镦（M1Ⅵ：5111）

A型铜镦（M1Ⅵ：5112）

2. C型（M1Ⅵ：5220）

1. B型（M1Ⅵ：5120）

3. D型（M1Ⅵ：3733）

铜镦

1. M1Ⅵ：5138　　　　　　　　　　　　　　　2. M1Ⅵ：5139

E型铜镦

1. M1Ⅵ：967　　2. M1Ⅵ：966　　3. M1Ⅵ：1863　　4. M1Ⅵ：5137

F型铜镦

1. F型镦（M1VI：5842）　　　　2. F型镦（M1VI：5843）　　　　4. H型镦（M1Ⅵ：5113）

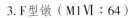

3. F型镦（M1Ⅵ：64）　　　　　　5. A型弩机（M1Ⅵ：2017）

铜镦、弩机

1. M1Ⅵ：5185

2. M1Ⅵ：5193

A型铜弩机

1. A型（M1VI：5191）　　　2. A型（M1VI：5478）　　　3. A型（M1VI：5479）

4. A型（M1VI：5481）　　　5. A型（M1VI：5540）　　　6. B型（M1VI：5467）

7. B型（M1VI：5469）　　　8. B型（M1VI：5222）　　　9. B型（M1VI：5462）

铜镞

1. B型（M1Ⅵ：5463）　　　2. B型（M1Ⅵ：5468）　　　3. B型（M1Ⅵ：5487）

4. B型（M1Ⅵ：5488）　　　5. B型（M1Ⅵ：5489）　　　6. C型（M1Ⅵ：5165）

7. C型（M1Ⅵ：5366）　　　8. C型（M1Ⅵ：5413）　　　9. D型（M1Ⅵ：5161）

铜镞

1. D型（M1Ⅵ：5325）

2. E型（M1Ⅵ：5163）

3. E型（M1Ⅵ：5505）

4. E型（M1Ⅵ：5500、M1Ⅵ：5506、M1Ⅵ：5504、M1Ⅵ：5502）

5. E型（M1Ⅵ：5499）

6. F型（M1Ⅵ：5166）

7. F型（M1Ⅵ：5434）

铜镞

1. G型（M1Ⅵ：5446）

2. G型（M1Ⅵ：5188）

3. G型（M1Ⅵ：5451）

4. H型（M1Ⅵ：5189）

6. H型（M1Ⅵ：5455、M1Ⅵ：5457、M1Ⅵ：5454）

5. H型（M1Ⅵ：5456）

7. I型（M1Ⅵ：5304）

8. I型（M1Ⅵ：5311）

铜镞

1. I型（M1Ⅵ：5308）

2. I型（M1Ⅵ：5528）

4. J型（M1Ⅵ：5255）

3. J型（M1Ⅵ：5258、M1Ⅵ：5261、M1Ⅵ：5260、M1Ⅵ：5256）

5. J型（M1Ⅵ：5262）

6. J型（M1Ⅵ：5264）

7. K型（M1Ⅵ：5245、M1Ⅵ：5242、M1Ⅵ：5241、M1Ⅵ：5239、M1Ⅵ：5158）

铜镞

1. K型（M1Ⅵ：5115）　　2. L型（M1Ⅵ：5123）　　3. L型（M1Ⅵ：5250、M1Ⅵ：5249、M1Ⅵ：5246）

4. L型（M1Ⅵ：5247）　　5. M型（M1Ⅵ：5157）　　6. M型（M1Ⅵ：5296）

7. M型（M1Ⅵ：5298）　　8. M型（M1Ⅵ：5155）　　9. M型（M1Ⅵ：5289）

铜镞

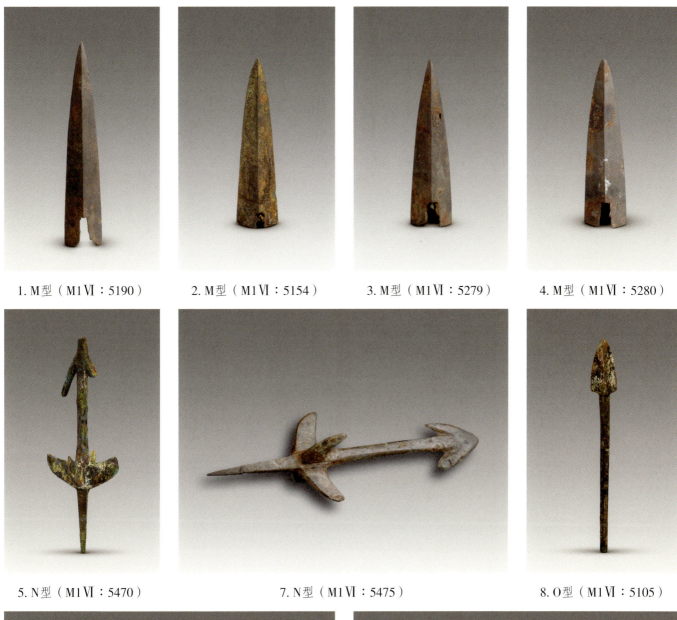

1. M型（M1Ⅵ：5190）　　2. M型（M1Ⅵ：5154）　　3. M型（M1Ⅵ：5279）　　4. M型（M1Ⅵ：5280）

5. N型（M1Ⅵ：5470）　　　　7. N型（M1Ⅵ：5475）　　　　8. O型（M1Ⅵ：5105）

6. N型（M1Ⅵ：5474）　　　　9. P型（M1Ⅵ：5200、M1Ⅵ：5209）

铜镞

1. A型箭箙包首饰（M1Ⅵ：5230）

2. A型箭箙包首饰（M1Ⅵ：5218）

3. A型承弓器（M1Ⅵ：5180）

4. A型承弓器（M1Ⅵ：5184）

铜箭箙包首饰、承弓器

1. A型（M1Ⅵ：3721）

2. A型（M1Ⅵ：3723）

3. B型（M1Ⅵ：3621）

铜承弓器

1. 盾饰（M1ⅥI：5109）

2. 盾饰（M1Ⅵ：5210）

3. 盾饰（M1Ⅵ：5228）

4. 盾饰（M1Ⅴ：5107）

5. 匕（M1Ⅵ：3794~M1Ⅵ：3796、M1Ⅵ：3885）

铜盾饰、匕

1. 箕形器（M1Ⅵ：5106）

2. A型削（M1Ⅵ：3792）

3. A型削（M1Ⅵ：3793）

铜箕形器、削

1. A型削（M1Ⅵ：3790）

4. C型带钩（M1Ⅵ：1119）

2. B型削（M1Ⅵ：3791）

3. B型削（M1Ⅵ：3789）

铜削、带钩

B型铜镇（M1Ⅵ：3821）

B型铜镇（M1Ⅵ：3822）

1. B型（M1Ⅵ：3823）

2. C型（M1Ⅵ：5144-1）

3. C型（M1Ⅵ：5144-2）

铜镇

1. M1Ⅵ：5144-3   2. M1Ⅵ：5144-4

B型铜镇

1. F型铺首（M1Ⅵ：5182）

2. F型铺首（M1Ⅵ：5192）

3. A型环（M1Ⅵ：1562）

4. A型环（M1Ⅵ：3798）

5. A型环（M1Ⅵ：5169）

6. A型环（M1Ⅵ：5131）

铜铺首、环

1. A型算珠形饰（M1Ⅵ：5168）　　2. A型算珠形饰（M1Ⅵ：5127）　　3. A型算珠形饰（M1Ⅵ：5170）

4. B型算珠形饰　　　　　5. B型算珠形饰　　　　　6. B型算珠形饰　　　　　7. B型算珠形饰
（M1Ⅵ：5201）　　　　（M1Ⅵ：5202）　　　　（M1Ⅵ：5203）　　　　（M1Ⅵ：5205）

8. C型算珠形饰（M1Ⅵ：3611、M1Ⅵ：5848、M1Ⅵ：5847、　　　　　9. 链饰（M1Ⅵ：5227）
　M1Ⅵ：1869、M1Ⅵ：1999）

铜算珠形饰、链饰

1. 铜构件（M1Ⅵ：3734）

2. 铜饰件（M1Ⅵ：3797）

3. 铜饰件（M1Ⅵ：3805）

4. 铜厄持（M1Ⅵ：1810）

5. 铜印章（M1Ⅵ：941）

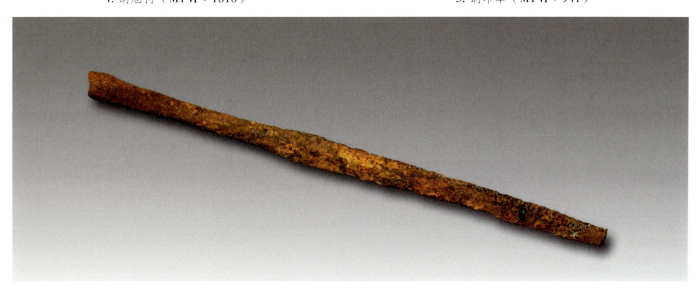

6. A型铁矛（M1Ⅵ：62）

铜构件、饰件、厄持、印章，铁矛

1. A型（M1Ⅵ：5081）　　　　　　　　　2. A型（M1Ⅵ：5122）

3. B型（M1Ⅵ：5083）

4. B型（M1Ⅵ：5084）

铁矛

1. A型戟（M1Ⅵ：5149）

2. 铍（M1Ⅵ：46）

3. 铍（M1Ⅵ：47）

4. 铩（M1Ⅵ：5151）

铁戟、铍、铩

1. A型剑（M1Ⅵ：5086）

3. A型镞（M1Ⅵ：5102）

2. 钩镶（M1Ⅵ：5134、M1Ⅵ：2018）

4. A型削（M1Ⅵ：1043）

铁剑、钩镶、镞、削

1. A型（M1Ⅵ：1048）

2. A型（M1Ⅵ：1118）

3. A型（M1Ⅵ：1815）

4. B型（M1Ⅵ：1010）

铁削

1. B型（M1Ⅵ：1041）

2. B型（M1Ⅵ：1117）

3. B型（M1Ⅵ：1120）

4. C型（M1Ⅵ：1008）

铁削

1. C型铁削（M1Ⅵ：1040）

2. C型铁削（M1Ⅵ：1116）

3. 铁环（M1Ⅵ：5224）

4. 铁环首器（M1Ⅵ：980）

5. 金构件（M1Ⅵ：4489、M1Ⅵ：4551、M1Ⅵ：3760）

6. 金兽首构件（M1Ⅵ：5221）

铁削、环、环首器，金构件、兽首构件

1. 圈饰（M1Ⅵ：5167）

2. 圈饰（M1Ⅵ：5171）

3. 圈饰（M1Ⅵ：5172）

4. 扣饰（M1Ⅵ：5174）

5. 箔饰（M1Ⅵ：5136）

金圈饰、扣饰、箔饰

2. M1Ⅵ：1812、M1Ⅵ：1561细部

1. M1Ⅵ：1812、M1Ⅵ：1561

3. M1Ⅵ：945

银伞柄箍饰

1. 盖弓帽（M1Ⅵ：55、M1Ⅵ：944、M1Ⅵ：942、M1Ⅵ：1820、M1Ⅵ：52、M1Ⅵ：1993）

3. 盖弓帽（M1Ⅵ：54）

4. A型镦（M1Ⅵ：1862）

2. A型镦（M1Ⅵ：5114）

5. B型镦（M1Ⅵ：975）

银盖弓帽、镦

1. 环（M1Ⅵ：1320）

2. 带钩（M1Ⅵ：940）

玉环、带钩

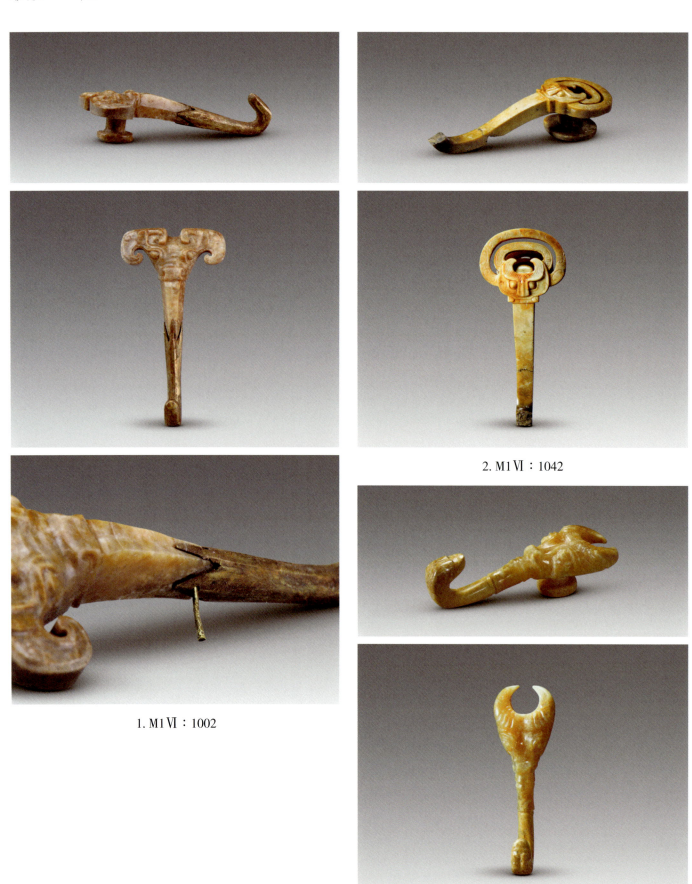

1. M1Ⅵ：1002

2. M1Ⅵ：1042

3. M1Ⅵ：1112

玉带钩

1. M1Ⅵ：1113

2. M1Ⅵ：1114

3. M1Ⅵ：1114细部放大　　　　　　　　　4. M1Ⅵ：1115

玉带钩

1. 玉带钩（M1Ⅵ：1752）

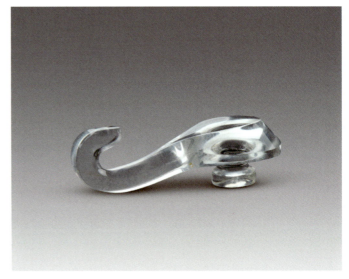

2. 石牌饰（M1Ⅵ：5223）　　3. 玛瑙珠饰（M1Ⅵ：5088）　　4. 水晶带钩（M1Ⅵ：1011）

5. 封泥（M1Ⅵ：4821）　　　　　　　　　6. 封泥（M1Ⅵ：5630）

玉带钩，石牌饰，玛瑙珠饰，水晶带钩，封泥

1. M1Ⅵ：5631

2. M1Ⅵ：5632

3. M1Ⅵ：5633

4. M1Ⅵ：5634

封泥

1. M1Ⅵ：5635

2. M1Ⅵ：5636

3. M1Ⅵ：5637

4. M1Ⅵ：5638

封泥

七A区上层出土遗物

1. 马络出土情况

2. 铜祖出土情况

七A区上层出土遗物

1. 铁削出土情况

2. 角笄出土情况

七A区上层出土遗物

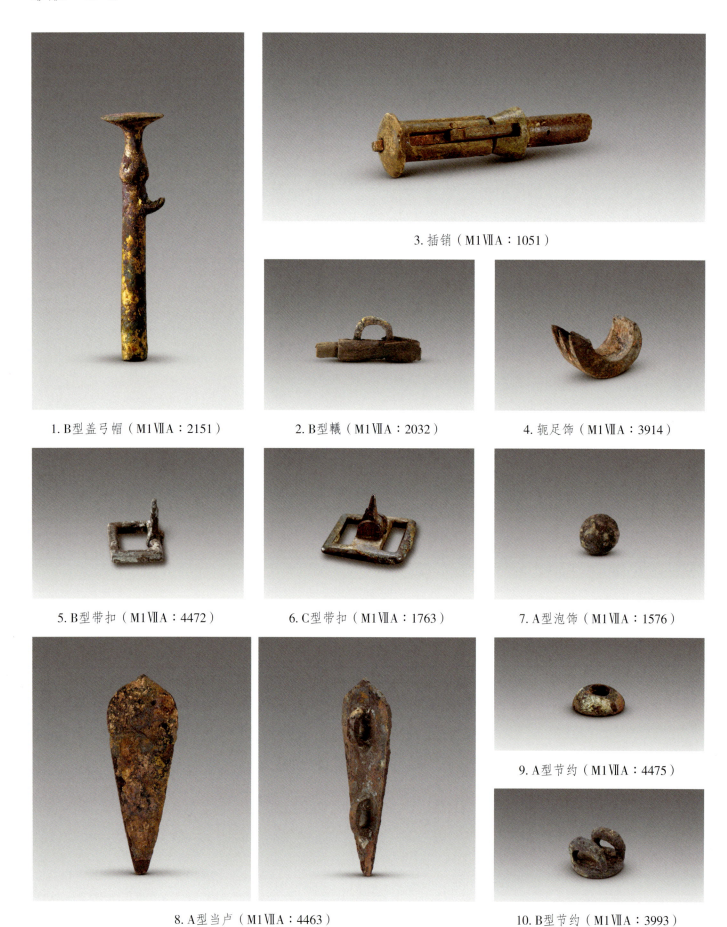

1. B型盖弓帽（M1ⅦA：2151）　　2. B型轙（M1ⅦA：2032）　　3. 插销（M1ⅦA：1051）

4. 轭足饰（M1ⅦA：3914）

5. B型带扣（M1ⅦA：4472）　　6. C型带扣（M1ⅦA：1763）　　7. A型泡饰（M1ⅦA：1576）

8. A型当卢（M1ⅦA：4463）

9. A型节约（M1ⅦA：4475）

10. B型节约（M1ⅦA：3993）

铜盖弓帽、轙、插销、轭足饰、带扣、泡饰、当卢、节约

1. G型镦（M1ⅦA：1065）

2. G型镦（M1ⅦA：1090）

3. A型环（M1ⅦA：1790）

4. 祖（M1ⅦA：66）

5. 祖（M1ⅦA：1053）

6. 构件（M1ⅦA：1052）

7. 构件（M1ⅦA：3916）

铜镦、环、祖、构件

1. F型（M1ⅦA：2026）

2. F型（M1ⅦA：2145、
M1ⅦA：2037、
M1ⅦA：2036、
M1ⅦA：2041）

3. G型（M1ⅦA：2034）

铜削

1. 银漏斗形器（M1ⅦA：67）

2. 银漏斗形器（M1ⅦA：68）

3. 玉带钩（M1ⅦA：939）

银漏斗形器，玉带钩

1. 笄（M1ⅧA：1563-1）

2. 笄（M1ⅧA：1563-2）细部

3. 觿（M1ⅧA：1064）

角笄、觿

七B区明器铜编钟、陶编磬与乐器架出土情况

1. 车軎（M1ⅦB：4441）

2. B型轙（M1ⅦB：1106）

3. A型帽饰（M1ⅦB：3665）

4. D型钩（M1ⅦB：2049）

5. D型泡饰（M1ⅦB：1952）

6. B型当卢（M1ⅦB：4442）

7. G型镦（M1ⅦB：3685）

铜车軎、轙、帽饰、钩、泡饰、当卢、镦

铜马络（M1ⅦB：2047）

第一套明器铜编钟

铜纽钟（M1ⅦB：4199）

铜甬钟（M1ⅦB：2459）

第二套明器铜编钟

铜纽钟（M1ⅦB：2524）

1. 甬钟（M1ⅦB：2456）

2. 销钉（M1ⅦB：2527）

铜甬钟、销钉

第三套明器铜编钟

铜纽钟（M1ⅦB：4192）

铜甬钟（M1ⅦB：4157）

1. 铜销钉（M1ⅦB：2504）

2. 铜销钉（M1ⅦB：4191）

3. 编钟架铜包边（M1ⅦB：1764-7、
　M1ⅦB：1764-8）

4. 铁鈹（M1ⅦB：1094）　　　　　　　5. E型铁削（M1ⅦB：2063）

铜销钉、编钟架包边，铁鈹、削

1. M1ⅦB：2455

2. M1ⅦB：2472

铜钲

1. M1ⅦB：2450

2. M1ⅦB：2451

3. M1ⅦB：2452

4. M1ⅦB：2453

5. M1ⅦB：2461

6. M1ⅦB：2462

陶编磬

1. M1ⅦB：2464

2. M1ⅦB：2465

3. M1ⅦB：2466

4. M1ⅦB：2467

5. M1ⅦB：2468

6. M1ⅦB：2469

陶编磬

1. M1ⅦB：2470

2. M1ⅦB：2481

3. M1ⅦB：2482

4. M1ⅦB：2483

5. M1ⅦB：2510

6. M1ⅦB：2511

陶编磬

1. M1ⅧB：2512

2. M1ⅧB：2513

3. M1ⅧB：2514

4. M1ⅧB：2516

5. M1ⅧB：2515

陶编磬

八区上层出土遗物

1. 伞柄箍饰（M1Ⅷ：1152）

2. B型帽饰（M1Ⅷ：1714）

3. B型帽饰（M1Ⅷ：1733）

4. B型帽饰（M1Ⅷ：2091）

5. 铜（M1Ⅷ：1699）

6. 铜（M1Ⅷ：1713）

7. 铜（M1Ⅷ：2079）

8. 兽首构件（M1Ⅷ：1121）

铜伞柄箍饰、帽饰、铜、兽首构件

1. 马蹄形管饰（M1Ⅷ：2100）   2. A型当卢（M1Ⅷ：25）

3. A型当卢（M1Ⅷ：44）   4. A型当卢（M1Ⅷ：1204）

5. A型节约（M1Ⅷ：2106）   6. A型节约（M1Ⅷ：2107）

铜马蹄形管饰、当卢、节约

1. B型弩机（M1Ⅷ：2076）

2. B型弩机（M1Ⅷ：1155）

3. B型弩机（M1Ⅷ：1697）

4. A型箭箙包首饰（M1Ⅷ：1186）

5. B型承弓器（M1Ⅷ：1153）

6. A型环（M1Ⅷ：34）

7. B型环（M1Ⅷ：37）

铜弩机、箭箙包首饰、承弓器、环

1. M1Ⅷ：45

2. M1Ⅷ：1123

铜虎帐座

九区上层铜虎帐座出土情况

1. B型盖弓帽（M1IX：1457）　　　2. B型盖弓帽（M1IX：1460）　　　3. A型帽饰（M1IX：1268）

4. 伞柄箍饰（M1IX：1454、M1IX：1581）　　　5. 伞柄箍饰（M1IX：1293、M1IX：1439、M1IX：1594）

铜盖弓帽、帽饰、伞柄箍饰

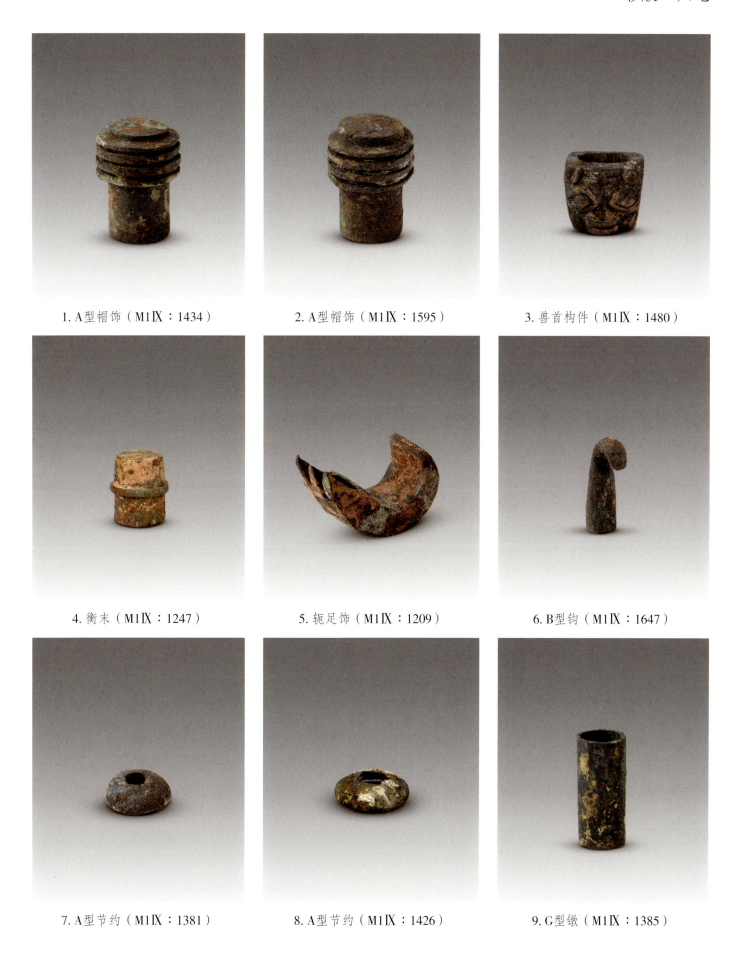

1. A型帽饰（M1IX：1434）　　2. A型帽饰（M1IX：1595）　　3. 兽首构件（M1IX：1480）

4. 衡末（M1IX：1247）　　5. 轭足饰（M1IX：1209）　　6. B型钩（M1IX：1647）

7. A型节约（M1IX：1381）　　8. A型节约（M1IX：1426）　　9. G型镦（M1IX：1385）

铜帽饰、兽首构件、衡末、轭足饰、钩、节约、镦

1. A型铜当卢（M1IX：1248）

2. B型铜承弓器（M1IX：1455）

3. B型铜承弓器（M1IX：1587）

4. B型铜环（M1IX：1628）

5. B型铁剑（M1IX：1746）

铜当卢、承弓器、环，铁剑

1. M1Ⅸ：1

2. M1Ⅸ：3

3. M1Ⅸ：5

铜虎帐座

十区上层出土马络

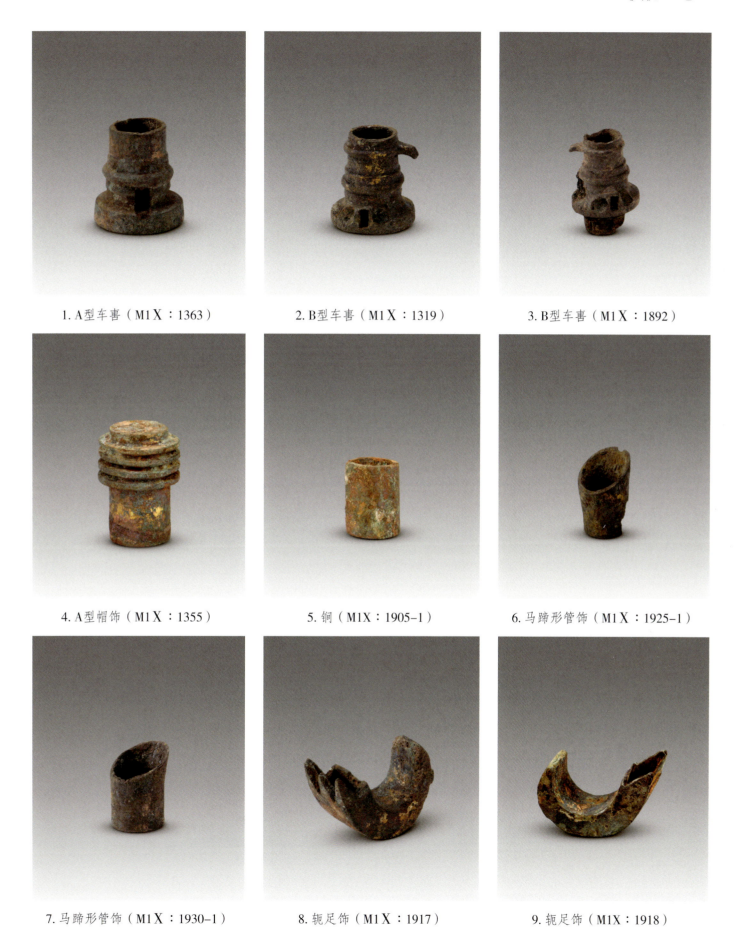

1. A型车軎（M1X：1363）　　　2. B型车軎（M1X：1319）　　　3. B型车軎（M1X：1892）

4. A型帽饰（M1X：1355）　　　5. 铜（M1X：1905–1）　　　6. 马蹄形管饰（M1X：1925–1）

7. 马蹄形管饰（M1X：1930–1）　　　8. 轭足饰（M1X：1917）　　　9. 轭足饰（M1X：1918）

铜车軎、帽饰、铜、马蹄形管饰、轭足饰

1. A型泡饰（M1X：1883）　　　　　　　　　2. A型当卢（M1X：1912）

3. D型镦（M1X：1905-2）　　　4. D型镦（M1X：1922-2）　　　5. D型镦（M1X：1930-2）

6. B型弩机（M1X：1907）　　　　　　　7. B型箭箙包首饰（M1X：1897）

铜泡饰、当卢、镦、弩机、箭箙包首饰

1. B型铜承弓器（M1X：1926）

2. A型铜带钩（M1X：1881）

3. A型铜带钩（M1X：1927）

4. C型铜环（M1X：3406）

5. C型铜环（M1X：3420）

6. 铁辖（M1X：1890）

7. A型铁钉（M1X：3414）

铜承弓器、带钩、环，铁辖、钉

西回廊下层出土遗物（由南向北）

东回廊下层出土遗物（由西向东）

1. 银沐盘及五支灯出土情况

2. 铜灯及铜虎出土情况

一区下层出土遗物

D型铜鼎（M1Ⅰ：3607）

1. D型鼎铭文（M1Ⅰ：3607）

2. 盆（M1Ⅰ：3748）

D型铜鼎铭文，铜盆

铜沐盘（M1 I ：3745）

1. M1 I ：3715

2. M1 I ：3716

铜缶

A型铜豆形灯（M1Ⅰ：3657）

A型铜豆形灯（M1Ⅰ：3659）

A型铜豆形灯（M1 Ⅰ：3654）

1. M1Ⅰ：3655

2. M1Ⅰ：3608

3. M1Ⅰ：3660

A型铜豆形灯

B型铜灯（M1Ⅰ：3653）

1. B型（M1 I：3656）

2. C型（M1 I：3648）

铜灯

1. C型（M1Ⅰ：3649）

2. D型（M1Ⅰ：3609）

铜灯

D型铜灯（M1 I：3609）

D型铜灯（M1Ⅰ：3609）

D型铜灯（M1Ⅰ：3645）

D型铜灯（M1Ⅰ：3645）

D型铜灯（M1Ⅰ：3645）

E型铜灯（M1Ⅰ：3707）

E型铜灯（M1 I ：3708）

F型铜灯（M1 I：3605）

1. M1 I：3605铭文

2. M1 I：3658

F型铜灯

铜虎

1. M1Ⅰ：3646、M1Ⅰ：3647

2. M1Ⅰ：3646

铜虎

铜虎（M1Ⅰ：3646）

铜虎（M1Ⅰ：3647）

1. 器盖（M1Ⅰ：3949）

2. C型铺首（M1Ⅰ：1664）

4. E型铺首（M1Ⅰ：3709）

5. A型环（M1Ⅰ：1663）

3. C型铺首（M1Ⅰ：1669）

铜器盖、铺首、环

1. 铜扣饰（M1 I ：3643）

2. 铁钩（M1 I ：3652-1、
M1 I ：3652-2）

3. 铁钳（M1 I ：3650、
M1 I ：3651）

铜扣饰，铁钩、钳

银沐盘（M1 I ：1766）

1. 石搓（M1Ⅰ：3601）

2. 石搓（M1Ⅰ：3602）

3. 石搓（M1Ⅰ：3603）

4. 漆沐盘（M1I：3744）

5. 灰陶搓（M1Ⅰ：3604）

6. 蜡（M1Ⅰ：3661）

石搓，漆沐盘，灰陶搓，蜡

二区下层出土铜编钟

铜编钟（M1Ⅱ：3917）

铜纽钟（M1Ⅱ：3917-8）

铜纽钟（M1Ⅱ：3917-8）

铜甬钟（M1Ⅱ：3917-18）

铜甬钟（M1Ⅱ：3917-18）

1. 编钟托架（M1：3917-26）正视

2. 编钟托架（M1：3917-26）

3. 编钟托架（M1：3917-26）侧视

4. 销钉（M1Ⅱ：3917-2）

铜编钟托架、销钉

银璧（M1Ⅱ：3917-29）

银璧（M1Ⅱ：3917-30）

银璧（M1Ⅱ：3917-31）

铜编钟底座（M1Ⅱ：3917-20）

1. 铜编钟底座（M1Ⅱ：3917–20）

2. A型琉璃珠（M1Ⅱ：3919）

铜编钟底座，琉璃珠

1. 编磬出土情况

2. 瑟枘及琉璃珠出土情况

三A区下层出土遗物

1. M1ⅢA：3918-1

2. M1ⅢA：3918-2

3. M1ⅢA：3918-3

4. M1ⅢA：3918-4

5. M1ⅢA：3918-5

6. M1ⅢA：3918-6

琉璃编磬

1. M1ⅢA：3918-7

2. M1ⅢA：3918-8

3. M1ⅢA：3918-9

4. M1ⅢA：3918-10

5. M1ⅢA：3918-11

6. M1ⅢA：3918-12

1. M1ⅢA：3918-13

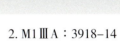

2. M1ⅢA：3918-14

3. M1ⅢA：3918-15

4. M1ⅢA：3918-16

5. M1ⅢA：3918-17

6. M1ⅢA：3918-18

琉璃编磬

1. 琉璃编磬（M1ⅢA：3918-19）

2. 琉璃编磬（M1ⅢA：3918-20）

3. 编磬铜包首（M1ⅢA：3918-23）

4. 编磬铜包首（M1ⅢA：3918-24）

琉璃编磬，铜包首

银璧（M1ⅢA：3918-26）

银璧（M1ⅢA：3918-27）

银璧（M1ⅢA：3918-28）

编磬铜底座（M1ⅢA：3918-21）

编磬铜底座（M1ⅢA：3918-21）

编磬铜底座（M1ⅢA：3918-21）细部

1. A型铜瑟枘（M1ⅢA：4066）

2. 金箔饰（M1ⅢA：4078）

3. 玉琴轸（M1ⅢA：4532、M1ⅢA：5076～M1ⅢA：5078）

4. 玉瑟枘（M1ⅢA：4073～
4076）

铜瑟枘，金箔饰，玉琴轸、瑟枘

1. A型玉瑟柱（M1ⅢA：3759、
   M1ⅢA：4071）

2. B型玉瑟柱（M1ⅢA：3754-1、
   M1ⅢA：4530、M1ⅢA：3756、
   M1ⅢA：3758）

3. B型玉瑟柱（M1ⅢA：3754-1）

4. B型玉瑟柱（M1ⅢA：3756）

5. B型琉璃珠（M1ⅢA：4072-7）

玉瑟柱，琉璃珠

1. 铜饰M1ⅢB：3705出土情况

2. A型铜琴枘（M1ⅢB：4064）

3. B型铜琴枘（M1ⅢB：4063）

4. 玉瑟柱（M1ⅢB：4461）

5. 玉瑟柱（M1ⅢB：4462）

6. A型琉璃珠（M1ⅢB：4061-16）

三B区下层出土遗物

1. C型瑟枘（M1ⅢB：4062）

2. 饰件（M1ⅢB：3705）

铜瑟枘、饰件

1. 四A区、四B区下层出土遗物

2. 灰陶钵与铜铃出土情况

四A区、四B区下层出土遗物

1. C型盖弓帽（M1ⅣA：3215）　　2. 兽首构件（M1ⅣA：3194）　　4. B型钩（M1ⅣA：3342）

5. B型钩（M1ⅣA：3181）　　6. A型带扣（M1ⅣA：3343）

3. 伞柄箍饰（M1ⅣA：3253）　　7. B型带扣（M1ⅣA：3334）　　8. B型节约（M1ⅣA：2958）

铜盖弓帽、兽首构件、伞柄箍饰、钩、带扣、节约

1. M1ⅣA：3096

2. M1ⅣA：2979

A型铜弩机

1. A型铜铃铛（M1ⅣA：3361、M1ⅣA：3362、M1ⅣA：3363）　　2. B型铜铃铛（M1ⅣA：3364、M1ⅣA：3365）

3. A型铜带钩（M1ⅣA：3304）

4. A型铜带钩（M1ⅣA：3303）

5. 铜衔环（M1ⅣA：3093）

6. 铁釭（M1ⅣA：3193）

7. 琉璃编磬（M1ⅣA：6027）

铜铃铛、带钩、衔环，铁釭，琉璃编磬

1. M1ⅣA：3368

2. M1ⅣA：3367

3. M1ⅣA：3369

灰陶钵

1. B型铜节约（M1ⅣB：2833）

2. G型铜镦（M1ⅣB：2909）

3. A型铜带钩（M1ⅣB：2829）

4. B型铁戟（M1ⅣB：2894）

5. B型铁戟（M1ⅣB：2895）

铜节约、镦、带钩，铁戟

五区下层出土遗物

1. A型车軎（M1Ⅴ：2667）

2. A型帽饰（M1Ⅴ：2703）

3. A型节约（M1Ⅴ：2692）

4. G型镦（M1Ⅴ：2784）

5. A型弩机（M1Ⅴ：2796）

6. O型镞（M1：2632）

7. O型镞（M1：5556）

8. A型带钩（M1Ⅴ：2655）

铜车軎、帽饰、节约、镦、弩机、镞、带钩

1. 出土遗物

2. 漆案出土情况

六区下层出土遗物

1. 出土漆案细部

2. 汲酒器及漆盘出土情况

六区下层出土遗物

1. 漆樽出土情况

2. 十一子漆奁出土情况

六区下层出土遗物

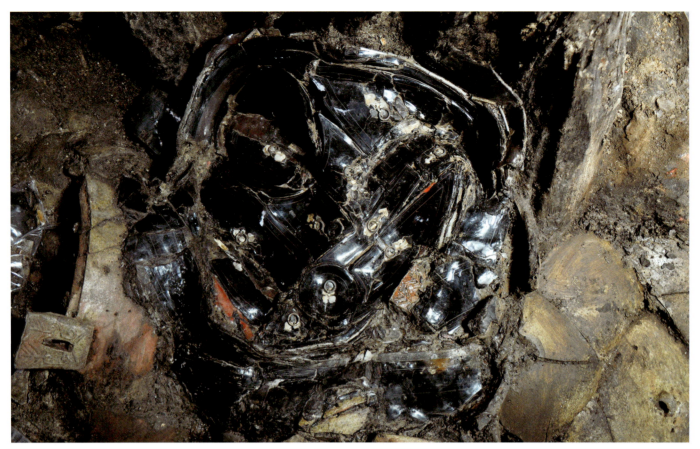

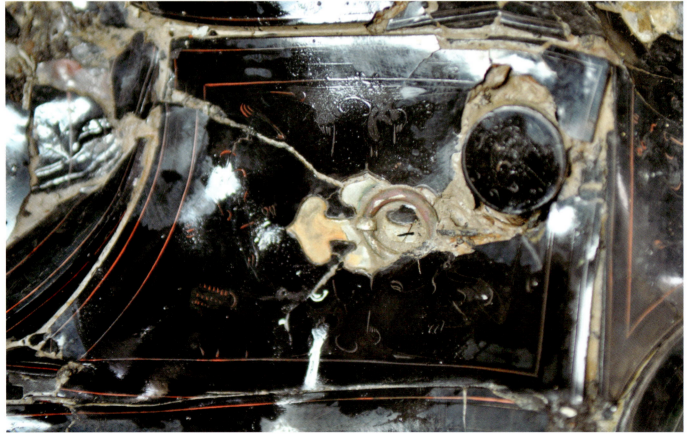

六区下层十一子漆奁出土情况

六区下层十一子漆奁出土情况

1. 十一子漆奁出土情况

2. 十一子漆奁及卮出土情况

六区下层出土遗物

六区下层铜明器出土情况

1. B型鼎（M1Ⅵ：3862）

2. B型锺（M1Ⅵ：3868）

3. B型锺（M1Ⅵ：3884）

4. C型锺（M1Ⅵ：3863）

铜鼎、锺

1. B型钫（M1Ⅵ：3865）

2. B型钫（M1Ⅵ：3866）

3. B型钫（M1Ⅵ：3874）

4. 匜（M1Ⅵ：3871）

铜钫、匜

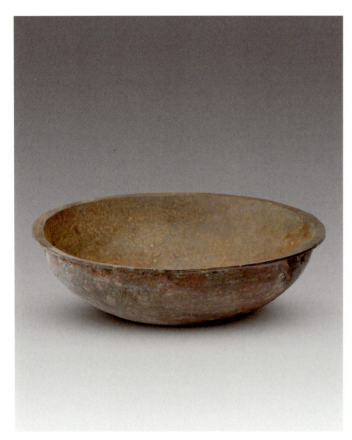

1. A型洗（M1Ⅵ：3899）

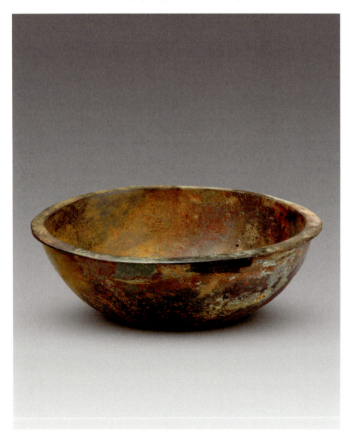

2. A型洗（M1Ⅵ：3900）

3. 瓢（M1Ⅵ：3875）

4. 瓢（M1Ⅵ：3875）铭文

5. B型勺（M1Ⅵ：3889）

铜洗、瓢、勺

2. 耳杯（M1Ⅵ：3880）

1. B型勺（M1Ⅵ：3890）

3. 染炉（M1Ⅵ：3740）

4. 染炉、耳杯（M1Ⅵ：3740、M1Ⅵ：3880）

铜勺、耳杯、染炉

1. M1Ⅵ：3967

2. M1Ⅵ：3968

铜鸠首柱形器

铜鸠首柱形器（M1Ⅵ：3968）细部（放大）

1. M1Ⅵ：3867

2. M1Ⅵ：3882

铜卮

1. M1Ⅵ：3956

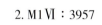

2. M1Ⅵ：3957

3. M1Ⅵ：3958

4. M1Ⅵ：3959

5. M1Ⅵ：3960

6. M1Ⅵ：3961

7. M1Ⅵ：4400

8. M1Ⅵ：4407

A型铜器座

1. A型器座（M1Ⅵ：4412）

2. B型器座（M1Ⅵ：3955）

3. D型铺首（M1Ⅵ：3951-1）

4. D型铺首（M1Ⅵ：3951-7）

5. 构件（M1Ⅵ：3895）

6. 扣饰（M1Ⅵ：3897）

铜器座、铺首、构件、扣饰

1. M1Ⅵ：3829

2. M1Ⅵ：3835

3. M1Ⅵ：3834

4. M1Ⅵ：3833

5. M1Ⅵ：3837

6. M1Ⅵ：4103

铜卮持

银洗（M1Ⅵ：3847）

1. M1Ⅵ：3848

2. M1Ⅵ：3849

3. M1Ⅵ：5643

银洗

银盘（M1Ⅵ：3980）

银盘（M1Ⅵ：3981）

石耳杯（M1Ⅵ：3879）

1. M1Ⅵ：3853   2. M1Ⅵ：3854

B型漆耳杯

1. M1Ⅵ：3855

2. M1Ⅵ：4711

B型漆耳杯

1. B型（M1Ⅵ：5059）内底纹饰

2. C型（M1Ⅵ：4714）

3. C型（M1Ⅵ：4715）

漆耳杯

D型漆耳杯（M1Ⅵ：4915）

1. M1Ⅵ：4628

3. M1Ⅵ：4631

2. M1Ⅵ：4656

4. M1Ⅵ：5057

E型漆耳杯外底铭文

1. M1Ⅵ：4633

2. M1Ⅵ：4633外底铭文

3. M1Ⅵ：4635

4. M1Ⅵ：4635外底铭文

E型漆耳杯

1. M1Ⅵ：4636外底铭文

2. M1Ⅵ：4637外底铭文

3. M1Ⅵ：4638

4. M1Ⅵ：4638外底铭文

E型漆耳杯

1. M1Ⅵ：4638

2. M1Ⅵ：4639外底铭文

3. M1Ⅵ：4641外底铭文

4. M1Ⅵ：4642外底铭文

E型漆耳杯

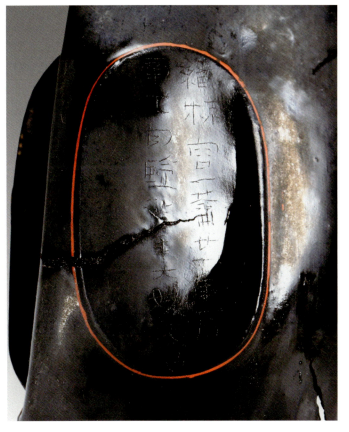

1. M1Ⅵ：4644外底铭文

2. M1Ⅵ：4645外底铭文

3. M1Ⅵ：4645、M1Ⅵ：4633

4. M1Ⅵ：4650外底铭文

E型漆耳杯

1. M1Ⅵ：4654

3. M1Ⅵ：4658

2. M1Ⅵ：4657

4. M1Ⅵ：4660

E型漆耳杯外底铭文

1. M1Ⅵ：4662

2. M1Ⅵ：4663

3. M1Ⅵ：4665

4. M1Ⅵ：4666

E型漆耳杯外底铭文

1. M1Ⅵ：4667

2. M1Ⅵ：4669

3. M1Ⅵ：4670

4. M1Ⅵ：4671

E型漆耳杯外底铭文

1. M1Ⅵ：4673

2. M1Ⅵ：4674

3. M1Ⅵ：4683

4. M1Ⅵ：4684

E型漆耳杯外底铭文

1. M1Ⅵ：4685

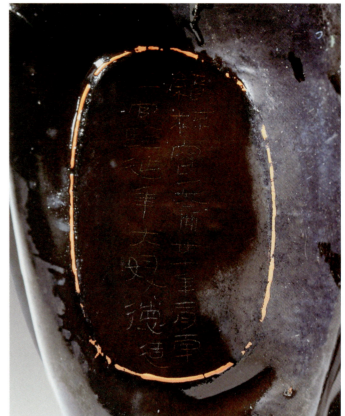

2. M1Ⅵ：4686

3. M1Ⅵ：4687

4. M1Ⅵ：4688

E型漆耳杯外底铭文

1. M1Ⅵ：4689

2. M1Ⅵ：4690

3. M1Ⅵ：4694

4. M1Ⅵ：4701

E型漆耳杯外底铭文

1. M1Ⅵ：4702

2. M1Ⅵ：4878

3. M1Ⅵ：4880

4. M1Ⅵ：4883

E型漆耳杯外底铭文

1. B型（M1Ⅵ：4624）

2. B型（M1Ⅵ：4823）

3. C型（M1Ⅵ：4723）

4. C型（M1Ⅵ：4723）底视

漆盘

1. C型（M1Ⅵ：4724）

2. C型（M1Ⅵ：4724）底视

3. C型（M1Ⅵ：4725）

4. D型（M1Ⅵ：4732）

漆盘

1. E型（M1Ⅵ：5065）

2. G型（M1Ⅵ：3954）

3. J型（M1Ⅵ：4413）

4. M1Ⅵ：5641铭文"中常食"

漆盘

1. J型（M1Ⅵ：5639）

2. M1Ⅵ：5639底视

3. M1Ⅵ：5640

4. MⅥ：5640细部

J型漆盘

1. M1Ⅵ：3910-1

2. M1Ⅵ：3910-2

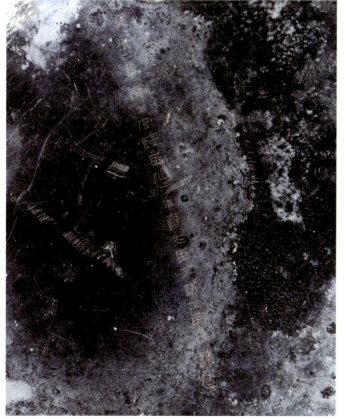

3. M1Ⅵ：3910-2底视

4. M1Ⅵ：3910-2俯视

B型漆卮

1. M1Ⅵ：3910-3

2. M1Ⅵ：3910-3外底

3. M1Ⅵ：3910-4

4. M1Ⅵ：3910-4器盖俯视

5. M1Ⅵ：3910-4外底

B型漆卮

1. M1Ⅵ：3912-1

2. M1Ⅵ：3912-1外底

3. M1Ⅵ：3912-2

4. M1Ⅵ：3912-2外底

B型漆卮

1. M1Ⅵ：3912-3

2. M1Ⅵ：3912-3

3. M1Ⅵ：3912-3外底

4. M1Ⅵ：3912-4

B型漆卮

1. M1Ⅵ：3912–4

2. M1Ⅵ：3912–4外底

3. M1Ⅵ：3912–5

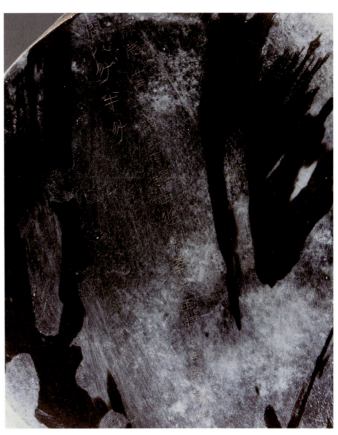

4. M1Ⅵ：3912–5

5. M1Ⅵ：3912–5外底

B型漆卮

1. M1Ⅵ：3912-6

2. M1Ⅵ：3912-6

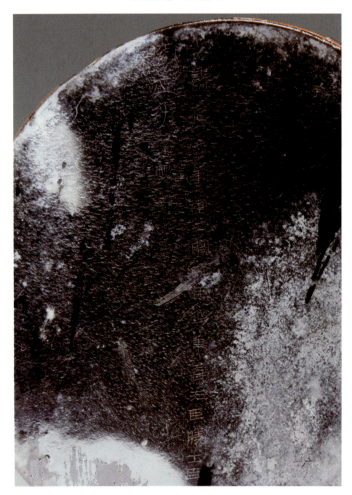

3. M1Ⅵ：3912-6外底

4. M1Ⅵ：3912-7

5. M1Ⅵ：3912-7外底

B型漆卮

1. M1Ⅵ：3912-8

2. M1Ⅵ：3912-9

3. M1Ⅵ：3912-10

4. M1Ⅵ：3912-10外底

B型漆卮

1. B型卮（M1Ⅵ：3912-11）

2. C型卮（M1Ⅵ：3826）

3. 樽（M1Ⅵ：3902）

4. 樽（M1Ⅵ：3902）细部

5. 盂（M1Ⅵ：3901）

6. 盂（M1Ⅵ：5845）

漆卮、樽、盂

1. 漆案

2. 铜足饰俯视

3. 铜足饰

漆案（M1Ⅵ：4414）

漆案铜足饰（M1Ⅵ：4414）

1. 筥（M1Ⅵ：4978）

4. 器盖（M1Ⅵ：3841）

2. 器盖（M1Ⅵ：3840）

5. 器盖（M1Ⅵ：3891）

6. 器盖（M1Ⅵ：3892）

3. 器盖（M1Ⅵ：3840）

7. 残器（M1Ⅵ：3810）

漆筥、器盖、残器

1. 漆器铭文残片"幸故"（M1Ⅵ：5058）

3. A型釉陶鼎（M1Ⅵ：3978）

2. A型釉陶鼎（M1Ⅵ：3970）

4. A型釉陶鼎（M1Ⅵ：3978）细部

漆器铭文残片"幸故"，A型釉陶鼎

1. M1Ⅵ：3984

2. M1Ⅵ：4100

3. M1Ⅵ：3986

4. M1Ⅵ：3986细部

A型釉陶鼎

1. A型（M1Ⅵ：3987）

2. A型（M1Ⅵ：4105）

3. B型（M1Ⅵ：4415）

4. B型（M1Ⅵ：4415）细部

釉陶鼎

1. M1Ⅵ：4401

2. M1Ⅵ：3979

3. M1Ⅵ：4101

4. M1Ⅵ：3973

B型釉陶鼎

1. M1Ⅵ：3969

2. M1Ⅵ：3976

3. M1Ⅵ：3983

4. M1Ⅵ：4416

B型釉陶鼎

1. M1Ⅵ：4104

2. M1Ⅵ：3985

3. M1Ⅵ：3972

4. M1Ⅵ：3975

B型釉陶鼎

1. M1Ⅵ：3977

2. M1Ⅵ：3971

3. M1Ⅵ：4106

B型釉陶鼎

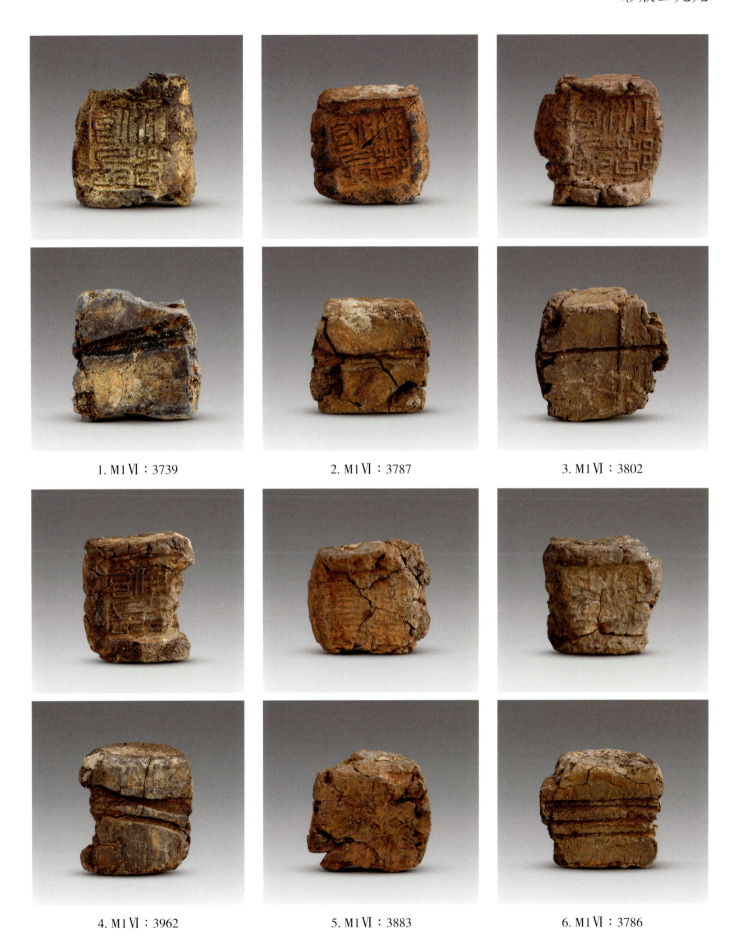

1. M1Ⅵ：3739　　　2. M1Ⅵ：3787　　　3. M1Ⅵ：3802

4. M1Ⅵ：3962　　　5. M1Ⅵ：3883　　　6. M1Ⅵ：3786

封泥

七A区下层出土遗物

1. 陶罐内出土果核

2. 陶罐内出土果核

3. 陶罐内出土蚌壳

七A区下层出土遗物

1. 陶罐内出土蚌壳

2. 银匜出土情况

七A区下层出土遗物

1. 铜厄持（M1ⅦA：3860）

2. 铜厄持（M1ⅦA：3906）

3. 铜厄持（M1ⅦA：3861）

4. 铜厄持（M1ⅦA：3858）

5. 铜厄持（M1ⅦA：3858）正视

6. 铜厄持（M1ⅦA：3859）

7. 铜厄持（M1ⅦA：3935）

8. 铁炉（M1ⅦA：3909）

铜厄持，铁炉

1. M1ⅦA：3812

2. M1ⅦA：3813

银匜

1. M1ⅦA：3814

2. M1ⅦA：3815

银匜

1. A型耳杯（M1ⅦA：4986）

2. A型耳杯（M1ⅦA：4987）

3. A型耳杯（M1ⅦA：4982）

4. A型卮（M1ⅦA：4984）

漆耳杯、卮

1. C型卮（M1ⅦA：4973）

2. 樽（M1ⅦA：3911）

3. 盂（M1ⅦA：4967）

4. 残器（M1ⅦA：3817）

漆卮、樽、盂、残器

1. 漆器（M1ⅦA：4988）

2. A型釉陶鼎（M1ⅦA：4110）

3. A型釉陶鼎（M1ⅦA：4119）

4. A型釉陶鼎（M1ⅦA：4122）

漆器，釉陶鼎

1. M1ⅦA：4118

2. M1ⅦA：4107

3. M1ⅦA：4111

4. M1ⅦA：4120

B型釉陶鼎

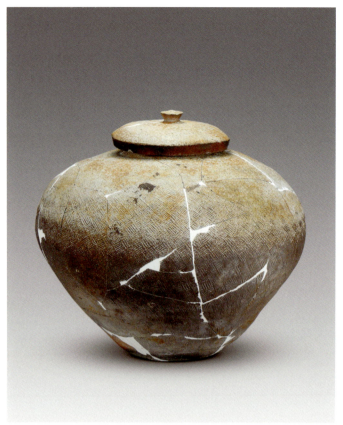

1. M1ⅦA：4114

3. M1ⅦA：4135

2. M1ⅦA：4117

4. M1ⅦA：4108

A型釉陶罐

1. A型（M1ⅦA：4109）

2. A型（M1ⅦA：4116）

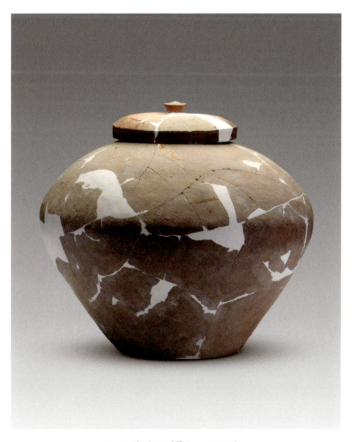

3. A型（M1ⅦA：4137）

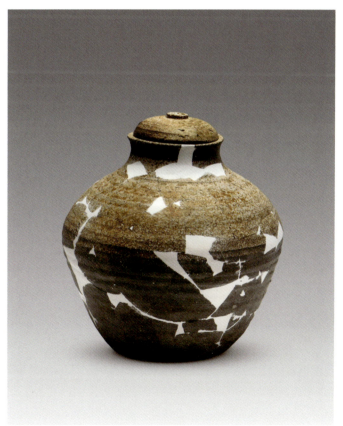

4. C型（M1ⅦA：4115）

釉陶罐

七B区下层出土遗物

七B区下层陶罐出土情况

1. M1ⅦB：4348

2. M1ⅦB：4352

3. M1ⅦB：4353

4. M1ⅦB：4354

B型铜鼎

1. M1ⅦB：4355

2. M1ⅦB：4357

3. M1ⅦB：4362

4. M1ⅦB：4356

B型铜鼎

1. M1ⅦB：4185

2. M1ⅦB：4346

3. M1ⅦB：4350

4. M1ⅦB：4363

C型铜鼎

1. C型鼎（M1ⅦB：4342）

2. C型鼎（M1ⅦB：4359）

3. D型锺（M1ⅦB：4186）

4. D型锺（M1ⅦB：4323）

铜鼎、锺

1. D型锺（M1ⅦB：4341）

2. D型锺（M1ⅦB：4309）

3. C型钫（M1ⅦB：4339）

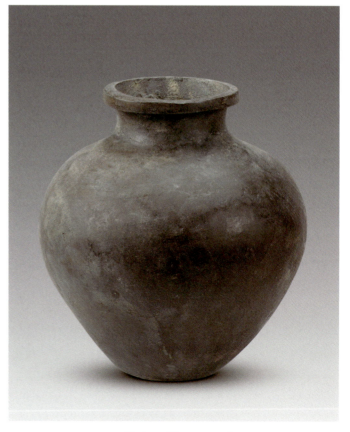

4. 罐（M1ⅦB：4313）

铜锺、钫、罐

1. 盉（M1ⅧB：4311）

3. 扣饰（M1ⅧB：4308）

4. 扣饰（M1ⅧB：4314）

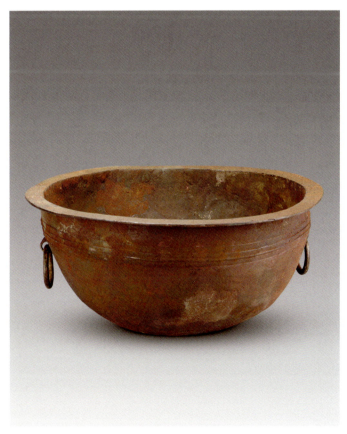

2. 盆（M1ⅧB：4349）

5. 扣饰（M1ⅧB：4316）

铜盉、盆、扣饰

1. 铜扣饰（M1ⅦB：4316）

2. 灰陶瓮（M1ⅦB：4174）

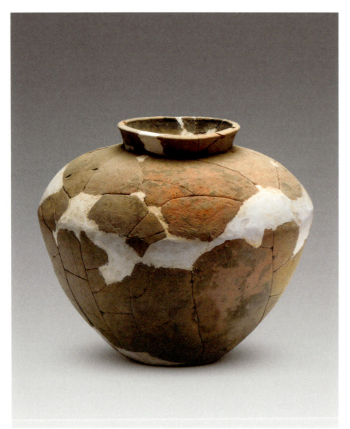

3. 灰陶瓮（M1ⅦB：5642）

4. A型釉陶鼎（M1ⅦB：4144）

铜扣饰，灰陶瓮，釉陶鼎

1. M1ⅧB：4131

2. M1ⅧB：4138

3. M1ⅧB：4169

4. M1ⅧB：4170

A型釉陶罐

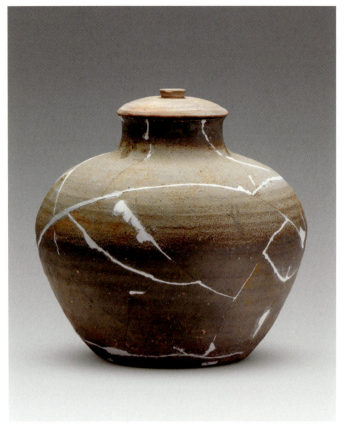

1. M1ⅦB：4126

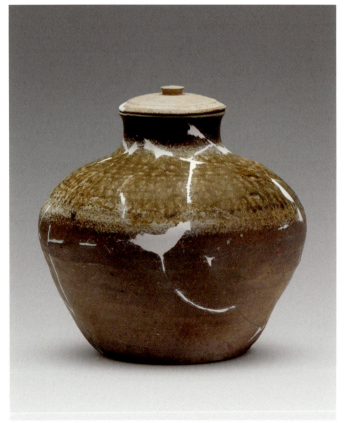

3. M1ⅦB：4127

2. M1ⅦB：4155

4. M1ⅦB：4132

B型釉陶罐

1. M1ⅦB：4133

2. M1ⅦB：4136

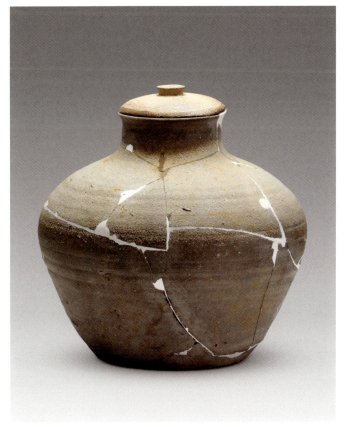

3. M1ⅦB：4140

4. M1ⅦB：4142

B型釉陶罐

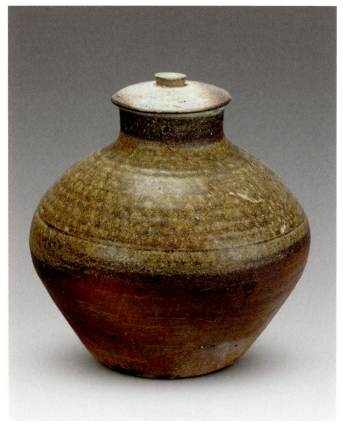

1. M1ⅧB：4145

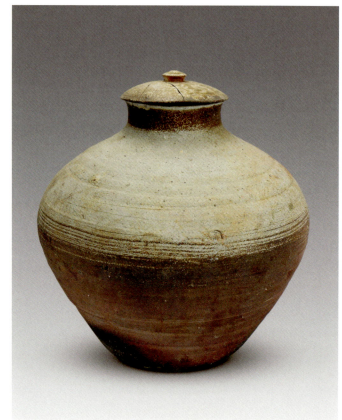

2. M1ⅧB：4146

3. M1ⅧB：4147

4. M1ⅧB：4152

B型釉陶罐

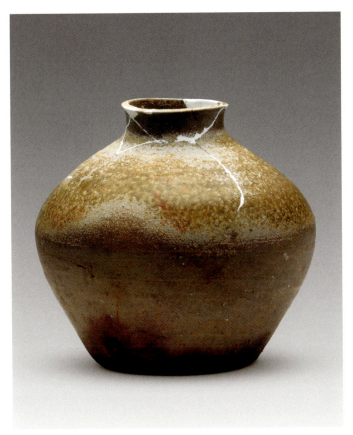

1. M1ⅦB：4160

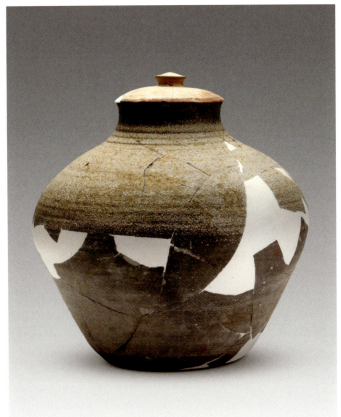

2. M1ⅦB：4161

3. M1ⅦB：4163

4. M1ⅦB：4165

B型釉陶罐

1. M1ⅦB：4166

2. M1ⅦB：4167

3. M1ⅦB：4168

4. M1ⅦB：4176

B型釉陶罐

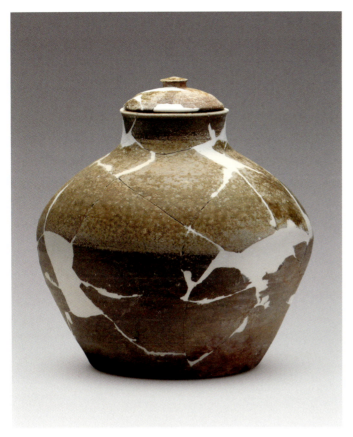

1. M1ⅦB：4177

2. M1ⅦB：4179

3. M1ⅦB：4180

4. M1ⅦB：4181

B型釉陶罐

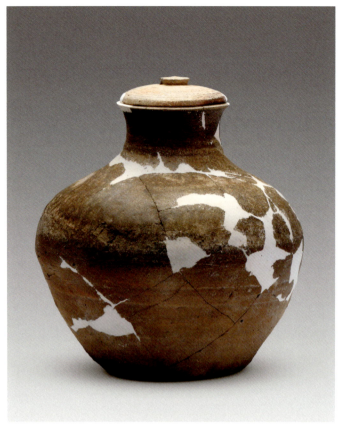

1. M1ⅦB：4347

2. M1ⅦB：4372

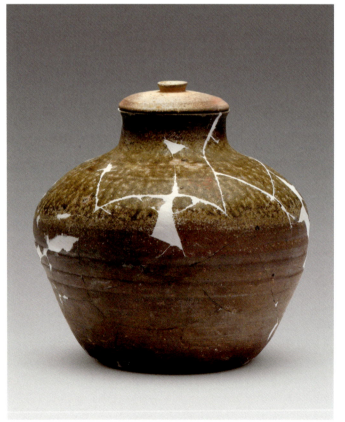

3. M1ⅦB：4374

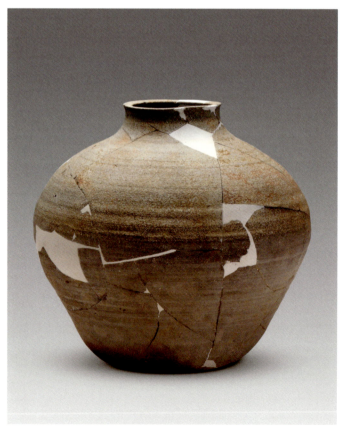

4. M1ⅦB：4376

B型釉陶罐

1. M1ⅦB：4379

2. M1ⅦB：4384

3. M1ⅦB：4385

4. M1ⅦB：4386

B型釉陶罐

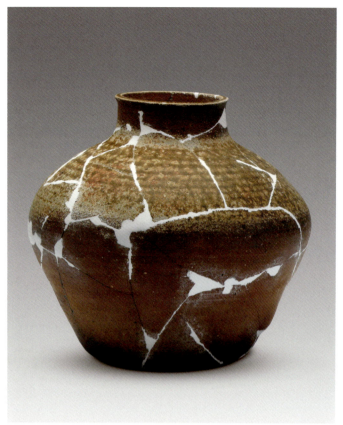

1. B型（M1ⅦB：4387）

2. C型（M1ⅦB：4153）

3. C型（M1ⅦB：4381）

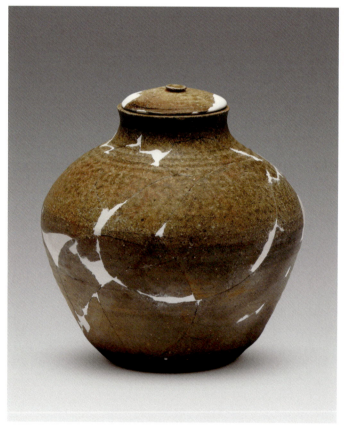

4. C型（M1ⅦB：4123）

釉陶罐

1. M1ⅧB：4124

2. M1ⅧB：4125

3. M1ⅧB：4128

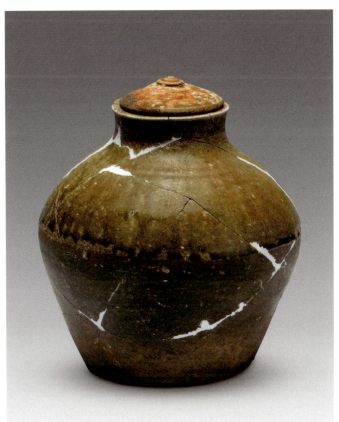

4. M1ⅧB：4130

C型釉陶罐

1. M1ⅦB：4134

3. M1ⅦB：4141

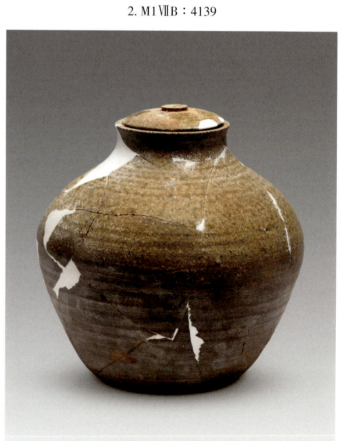

2. M1ⅦB：4139

4. M1ⅦB：4148

C型釉陶罐

1. M1ⅦB：4149

2. M1ⅦB：4150

3. M1ⅦB：4151

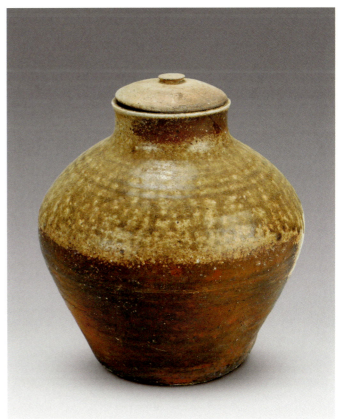

4. M1ⅦB：4154

C型釉陶罐

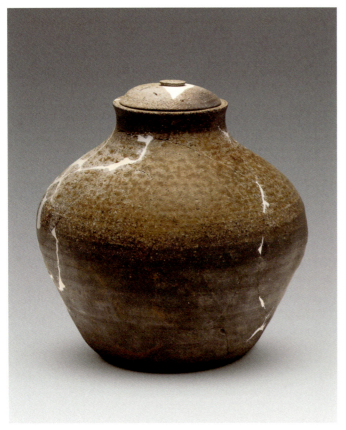

1. M1ⅦB：4156

2. M1ⅦB：4157

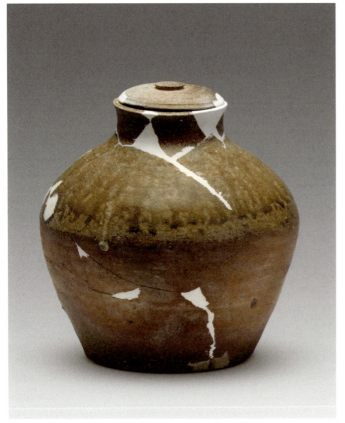

3. M1ⅦB：4158

4. M1ⅦB：4159

C型釉陶罐

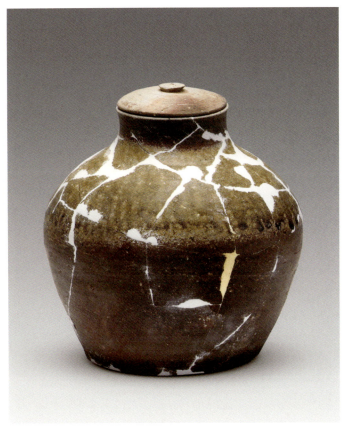

1. M1ⅦB：4162

2. M1ⅦB：4164

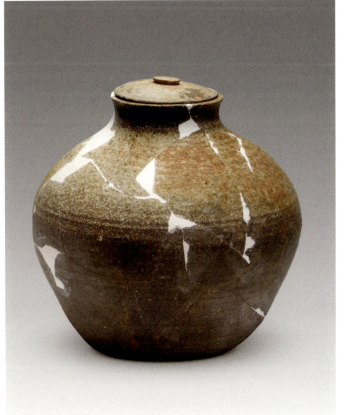

3. M1ⅦB：4171

4. M1ⅦB：4375

C型釉陶罐

1. 出土遗物

2. 铜鼎、銷、甑出土情况

八区下层出土遗物

1. 铜鐁出土情况

2. D型铜鼎（M1Ⅷ：4226）

八区下层出土遗物

E型铜鼎（M1Ⅷ：4225）

铜鋗（M1Ⅷ：4229）

1. 銷（M1Ⅷ：4227）

2. 壺（M1Ⅷ：4256）

3. 壺（M1Ⅷ：4257）

4. 壺（M1Ⅷ：4224）

铜銷、壶

铜鐽（M1Ⅷ：4302）

1. B型釜（M1Ⅷ：4228）

2. 釜、甑组合（ M1Ⅷ：4230、M1Ⅷ：4242）

3. B型釜（M1Ⅷ：4230）

4. 釜、甑组合（M1Ⅷ：4219、M1Ⅷ：4220）

铜釜、甑

1. C型釜（M1Ⅷ：4219）

2. 甑（M1Ⅷ：4221）

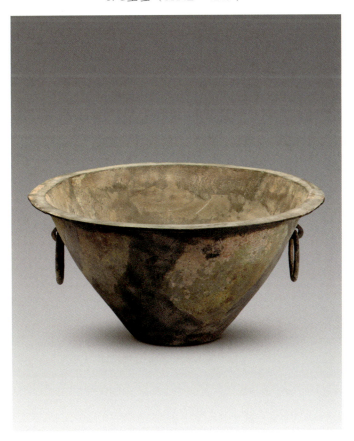

3. 甑（M1Ⅷ：4242）

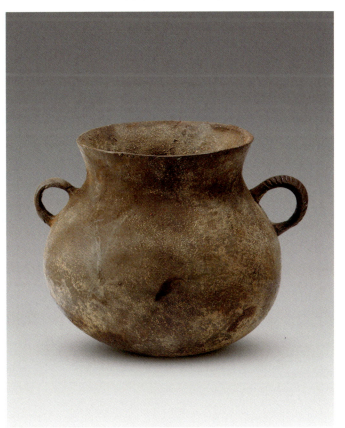

4. 鍪（M1Ⅷ：4304）

铜釜、甑、鍪

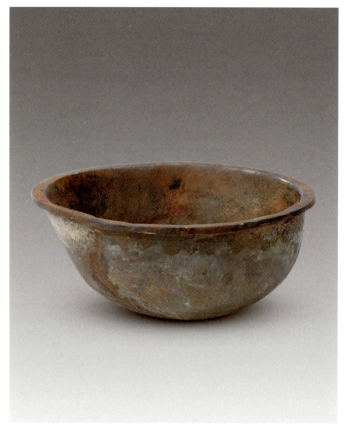

1. A型洗（M1Ⅷ：4262）

2. A型洗（M1Ⅷ：4263）

3. B型勺（M1Ⅷ：4244）

4. B型勺（M1Ⅷ：4245）

5. B型勺（M1Ⅷ：4252）

铜洗、勺

1. B型勺（M1Ⅷ：4258）

2. C型勺（M1Ⅷ：4488）

3. C型勺（M1Ⅷ：4250）

4. 盒（M1Ⅷ：4211）

5. 扣饰（M1Ⅷ：5645-1、M1Ⅷ：5645-2）

6. 扣饰（M1Ⅷ：5646-1、M1Ⅷ：5646-2）

铜勺、盒、扣饰

1. M1Ⅷ：5647-1、M1Ⅷ：5647-2

2. M1Ⅷ：5647-1铭文

3. M1Ⅷ：4255

4. M1Ⅷ：4253

5. M1Ⅷ：4254

铜扣饰

1. 铁炉（M1Ⅷ：4222）

2. A型釉陶罐（M1Ⅷ：4217）

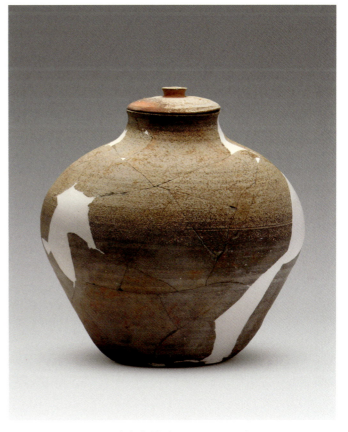

3. B型釉陶罐（M1Ⅷ：4207）

铁炉，釉陶罐

1. A型釉陶壶（M1Ⅷ：4210）

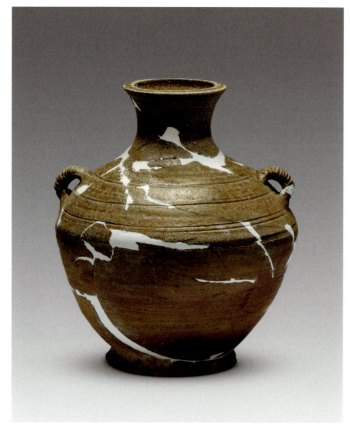

2. B型釉陶壶（M1Ⅷ：4201）

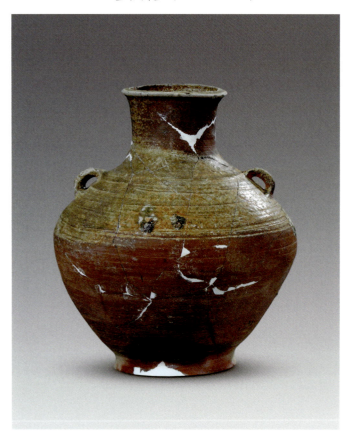

3. B型釉陶壶（M1Ⅷ：4215）

4. 釉陶瓮（M1Ⅷ：4213）

釉陶壶、瓮

1. M1Ⅷ：4204

2. M1Ⅷ：4208

3. M1Ⅷ：4209

4. M1Ⅷ：4214

釉陶瓮

1. M1Ⅷ：4216

2. M1Ⅷ：4218

3. M1Ⅷ：4202

釉陶瓮

九区下层铜钱出土情况

九区下层漆器出土情况

A型铜釜（M1IX：4261）

A型铜釜（M1IX：4240）

1. M1Ⅸ：4241

2. M1Ⅸ：5629

A型铜釜

1. A型釜（M1Ⅸ：4233）

2. 厄持（M1Ⅸ：3561）

3. 钱（M1Ⅸ：4249）

4. 钱（M1Ⅸ：4249）

铜釜、厄持、钱

A型漆盘（M1Ⅸ：3569）

A型漆盘（M1IX：3567）

H型漆盘（M1Ⅸ：4742）

I型漆盘（M1IX：5849）

1. B型罐（M1Ⅸ：4206）

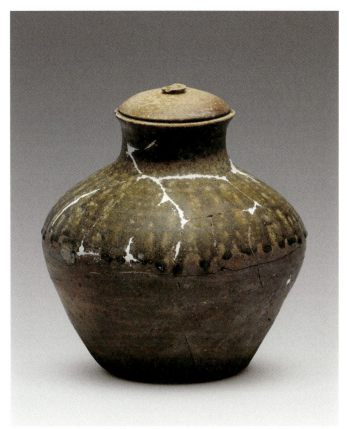

2. C型罐（M1Ⅸ：4235）

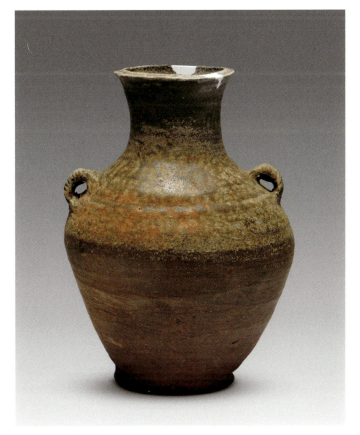

3. A型壶（M1Ⅸ：4237）

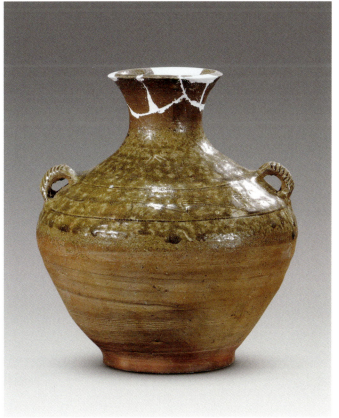

4. B型壶（M1Ⅸ：4239）

釉陶罐、壶

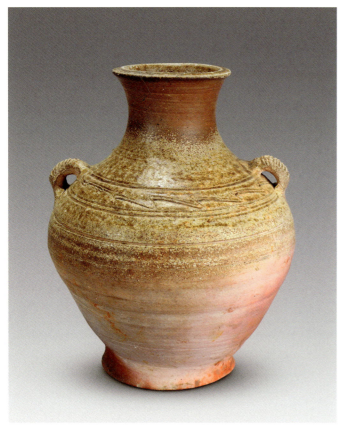

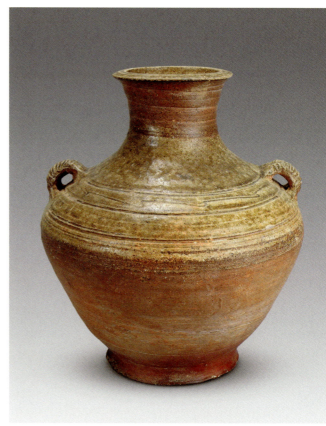

1. B型壶（M1IX：4236）

2. B型壶（M1IX：4205）

3. 瓮（M1IX：4200）

4. 瓮（M1IX：4238）

釉陶罐、瓮

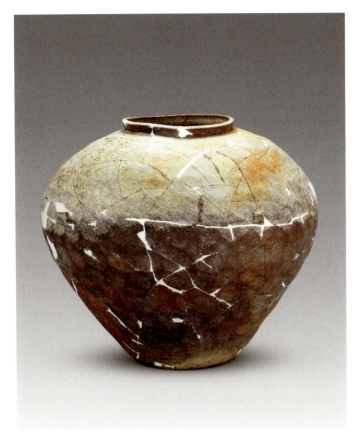

1. 釉陶瓮（M1Ⅸ：4203）

2. B型铜带扣（M1Ⅹ：3533）

3. A型铜当卢（M1Ⅹ：4503）

4. 铜马衔镳（M1Ⅹ：3467）

5. B型铜箭箙包首饰（M1Ⅹ：3535）

釉陶瓮，铜带扣、当卢、马衔镳、箭箙包首饰

1. B型铜承弓器（M1X：3529）

2. 铜构件（M1X：3553）

3. 铁马衔镳（M1X：1343）

铜承弓器、构件，铁马衔镳

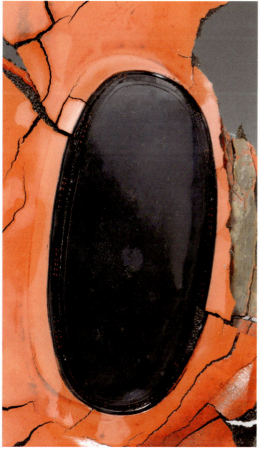

A型漆耳杯（M1X：4598）

A型漆耳杯（M1Ⅹ：4870）

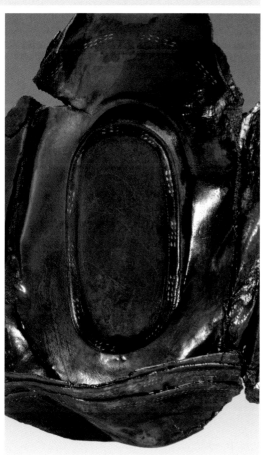

C型漆耳杯（M1X：4940）

A型漆盘（M1X：3577）

1. 铜衡末（M1XI：2581）

2. B型铜节约（M1XI：2612）

3. 铁铜（M1XI：619）

4. 铜承弓器（M1XI：401）

5. 铁"T"形器（M1XI：395）

6. C型铜盖弓帽（M1XII：2540）

7. A型铜带扣（M1XII：2592）

8. B型铜带扣（M1XIII：2320）

铜衡末、节约、承弓器、盖弓帽、带扣，铁铜、"T"形器

1.构件（M1ⅩⅡ：2578）

3.马衔镳（M1ⅩⅢ：2215）

4.马衔镳（M1ⅩⅢ：2278）

2.D型泡饰（M1ⅩⅢ：2227）

5.C型节约（M1ⅩⅢ：2217）

铜构件、泡饰、马衔镳、节约

1. C型节约（M1XⅢ：2336）

2. G型镦（M1XⅢ：2194）

3. A型带钩（M1XⅢ：2187）

4. 构件（M1XⅢ：2291）

5. 构件（M1XⅢ：2295）

6. 构件（M1XⅢ：2190）

7. 构件（M1XⅢ：5846）

铜节约、镦、带钩、构件

1. B型铁剑（M1ⅩⅢ：2319）

2. C型铜盖弓帽（M1ⅩⅣ：2340）

3. B型铜轙（M1ⅩⅣ：2448）

4. 铜衡末（M1ⅩⅣ：2434）

5. A型铜节约（M1ⅩⅣ：2376）

6. B型铜节约（M1ⅩⅣ：2250）

7. C型铜节约（M1ⅩⅣ：2380）

铁剑，铜盖弓帽、轙、衡末、节约

1. G型铜镦（M1ⅩⅣ：2247）

2. C型铜环（M1ⅩⅣ：2361）

3. 铁马衔镳（M1ⅩⅣ：2354）

4. A型铁钉（M1ⅩⅣ：2428）

铜镦、环，铁马衔镳、钉

Excavation Report on the King of Jiangdu's Tomb M1

of the Western Han Period at Dayunshan

(Abstract)

The tomb of King of Jiangdu is located on the top of Mount Dayun, Yunshan Village, Xuyi County, and is in the central region of Jiangsu Province. It is 73. 6 meters high, 30 kilometers to the west of Xuyi county seat, 1 kilometer to the south of Dongyang Site (Han Dynasty), and next to Mount Qingdun and Mount Xiaoyun cemeteries in southwest.

From September 2009 to December 2012, archaeologists from Nanjing Museum did exploration and salvage excavation, found a complete cemetery of King of Jiangdu of the Western Han Dynasty, and unearthed a great quantity of pottery, bronze, gold and silver, jade and lacquer objects, the total is over 10, 000 in number (set) .

There are three main graves (M1、M2、M8), 11 attendant graves (M3—M6, M9—M15), 2 horse and chariot pits (K2 and K7), 2 weapon pits (K3 and K6) in the whole cemetery. Main graves and horse and chariot pits locate in the south, attendant graves and weapon pits locate in the north, all the graves are in orderly and precise arrangement. In this report, we present the tomb M1.

Tomb M1 assumes the shape of a Chinese character – 中, its coffin chamber is a wooden structure names Huangchangticou, including outer corridor, anteroom, middle corridor, inner corridor, and inner chamber, outer and inner coffins. Even though has been robbed, more than 8, 000 objects such as pottery, bronze, gold and silver, jade and lacquer were unearthed from this grave.

From all sides like tomb layout, norm, structure, jade ornamented coffin and jade burial suits, high grade tomb objects, we believe that the occupant of tomb M1 is a king in the Western Han Dynasty. And inscriptions on the objects reveal the name of the principality and its particular year. Then we ascertain the specific identity of this grave, he is Liu Fei, the first generation of Jiangdu King, also the master of Tomb of Mount Dayun.

Tomb objects from tomb M1 have tremendous information which helps archaeologists to research the system of Kings' cemetery and the use of jade in early stage of the Western Han Dynasty, and also provides new thoughts and ways to study Han period archaeology.